Rembrandt and His Time

SELECTED PAINTINGS

LAURIE WINTERS, DAVID DE WITT, AND MARY WEAVER CHAPIN

MILWAUKEE ART MUSEUM

Rembrandt and His Time: Selected Paintings was published on the occasion of
the exhibition *Rembrandt and His Time: Masterworks from the Albertina, Vienna,* on view
at the Milwaukee Art Museum from October 8, 2005 through January 8, 2006.

First Edition
© 2005 Milwaukee Art Museum
700 North Art Museum Drive
Milwaukee, Wisconsin 53202

All rights reserved under International and Pan-American Copyright Conventions.
Except for legitimate excerpts customary in review or scholarly publications, no part of this
publication may be reproduced or transmitted in any form or by any means, electronic or
mechanical, including photocopying, recording, or information storage or retrieval systems,
without permission in writing from the publisher.

Published by the Milwaukee Art Museum

Coordinator and Editor: Terry Ann R. Neff, t.a. neff associates, inc., Tucson, Arizona
Designer: Steve Biel, Milwaukee Art Museum
Printed and bound by Friesens, Canada

Winters, Laurie.
    Rembrandt and his time : selected paintings / Laurie Winters, David
de Witt, and Mary Weaver Chapin. -- 1st ed.
        p. cm.
    "Published on the occasion of the exhibition Rembrandt and His Time:
Masterworks from the Albertina, Vienna, on view at the Milwaukee
Art Museum from October 8, 2005 through January 8, 2006."
    Includes bibliographical references and index.
    ISBN 0-944110-74-6 (alk. paper)
    1. Painting, Dutch--17th century--Exhibitions. 2. Rembrandt
Harmenszoon van Rijn, 1606-1669--Exhibitions.   I. De Witt, David.
II. Chapin, Mary Weaver. III. Graphische Sammlung Albertina.
IV. Milwaukee Art Museum. V. Title.
ND636.W56 2005
759.9492'09'03207477595--dc22
                                        2005022030

FRONT COVER: Rembrandt Harmensz. van Rijn, *Landscape with the Good Samaritan*, 1638
(cat. no. 4, detail)
BACK COVER: Willem van de Velde the Younger, *Seascape*, c. 1660 (cat. no. 15)
FRONTISPIECE: Ludolf Bakhuizen, *Fishing Vessels Offshore in Heavy Seas*, 1684 (cat. no. 14, detail)
ILLUSTRATION: Adrian van Ostade, *"Le Ménétrier" (The Violinist)*, 1673 (cat. no. 7, detail)

Contents

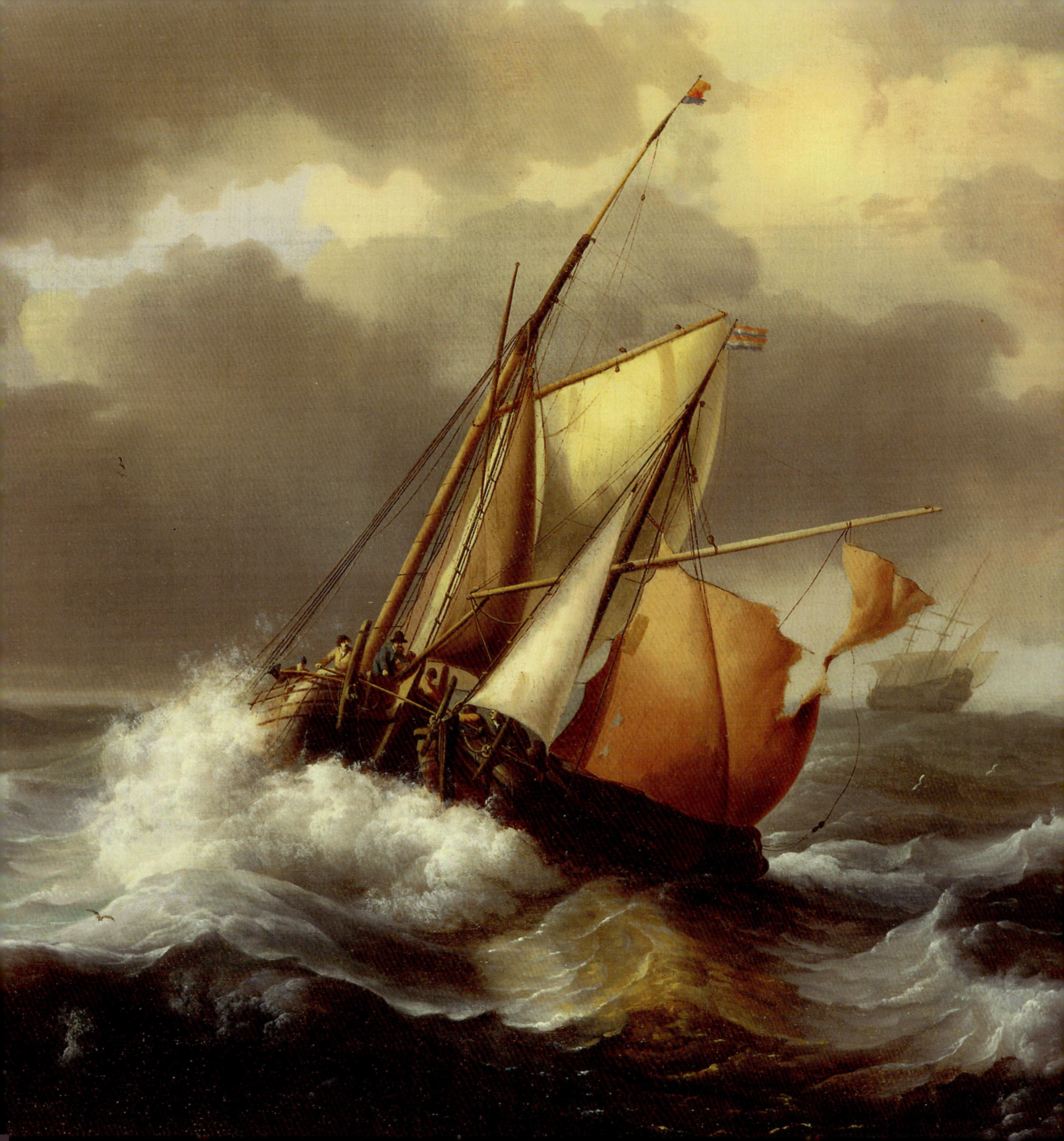

FOREWORD

DAVID GORDON

DIRECTOR, MILWAUKEE ART MUSEUM

The exhibition *Rembrandt and His Time* presents the seminal work of one of the world's greatest artists to American audiences in conjunction with Rembrandt's 400th anniversary celebration in 2006. Rembrandt's unique humanity and immediacy of touch—in landscapes, genre scenes, and biblical and mythological subjects—has remained accessible to viewers through the centuries. His drawings and prints are remarkable for their keen sense of observation combined with soaring leaps of the imagination. We are delighted to bring this spirit of excellence and imagination to the Milwaukee Art Museum.

We are doubly pleased that this important project was developed as part of an ongoing collaboration with the Albertina that has much promise for the future. I am especially grateful to its director, Klaus Albrecht Schröder, for his initial conception of the exhibition and his essential support throughout all stages of its development. The combined efforts of our mutual institutions have resulted in an exhibition of the highest standards. *Rembrandt and His Time* features a selection of 112 works on paper from the Albertina. It also has fifteen related paintings from museums and private collectors around the world that demonstrate the varied connections and ways of thinking about drawings and paintings in the seventeenth century. Among the paintings is Rembrandt's spectacular *Landscape with the Good Samaritan*, which was lent by the Czartoryski Museum in Cracow, as part of a continuing informal cultural exchange with the Milwaukee Art Museum.

We owe special thanks to Marian Bisanz-Prakken, curator of Netherlandish drawings at the Albertina, and to Laurie Winters, curator of earlier European art at the Milwaukee Art Museum, for their enormous contributions in shaping the content of the exhibition and the two accompanying catalogues. The first and larger book features the masterworks from the Albertina; the smaller, supplementary catalogue presents the paintings in the exhibition, for which Laurie Winters has been primarily responsible.

For their generous support of this exhibition, I would like to extend my gratitude to the presenting sponsor We Energies and to Christopher Seton Abele of the Argosy Foundation. We are genuinely grateful to these sponsors for helping us share Rembrandt's unique vision of the human experience with a broad audience. This exhibition has also earned the support of the National Endowment for the Humanities, and we are pleased to convey our gratitude in particular to Chairman Dana Gioia and to Indemnity Administrator Alice Whelihan for assisting us in bringing these works to the United States.

SPONSORS' STATEMENTS

GALE KLAPPA, CHAIRMAN AND CHIEF EXECUTIVE OFFICER
WISCONSIN ENERGY CORPORATION

CHRIS ABELE, CHIEF EXECUTIVE OFFICER
ARGOSY FOUNDATION

Wisconsin Energy Foundation is pleased to support the world-class exhibition *Rembrandt and His Time*, which brings from Vienna to Milwaukee the rich diversity of the Albertina's Netherlandish collections. The Albertina has one of the finest collections of works on paper in the world. Its holdings travel only infrequently, and then usually to museums in major cities globally. Supplementing the Albertina works are fifteen related paintings gathered from museums and private collections around the world. For this important exhibition, Milwaukee is the sole venue.

The exhibition is intended to help launch the celebration of the 400th anniversary of Rembrandt's birth in 2006. We are excited about working with the Milwaukee Art Museum to bring the work of an artist of Rembrandt's stature to the United States and to share with the people of our city the rich tradition of seventeenth-century Dutch art.

The Wisconsin Energy Foundation believes that partnering with the Milwaukee Art Museum on significant exhibitions is of mutual benefit. Art enhances the quality of life, and first-rate cultural offerings add great value to the community, the area, and the state. In the case of an international exhibition such as *Rembrandt and His Time*, the communal benefits have international resonance.

The opportunity to work with the Milwaukee Art Museum in bringing exhibitions of excellence to Milwaukee has been extremely rewarding. *Rembrandt and His Time* continues this experience through an extraordinary display of important works by remarkable artists from the Golden Age in Holland. Rembrandt was a pivotal and crowning figure in the evolution of Dutch seventeenth-century painting and drawing. To dramatically break with stylistic tradition takes courage; to do so with such confidence and aplomb as to establish new traditions takes even more.

Rembrandt's work is characterized by his dynamic depiction of light and extraordinarily rich palette. To conventional portraiture, he added an uncanny ability to capture complex personality and character. All of this he did with apparently intuitive technique, visible in his spontaneous, swift strokes of pen or brush, finely detailed etching, or fluid application of paint. His work reflects his interest in all aspects of his world, offering a glimpse into the human condition through landscape, portraits, biblical and mythological subjects, and the everyday activities of life. This exhibition is a window on an exceptional talent and the Argosy Foundation is proud to support it.

ACKNOWLEDGMENTS

LAURIE WINTERS

CURATOR OF EARLIER EUROPEAN ART, MILWAUKEE ART MUSEUM

The seed for this exhibition was sown in conversations with Albertina Director Klaus Albrecht Schröder about collaborations between our two institutions. Director David Gordon in Milwaukee wholeheartedly embraced the idea of continuing international collaboration. Originally conceived as a show of masterpieces, the exhibition almost immediately evolved into a more serious look at the work of Rembrandt and his contemporaries that would help launch the 400th anniversary celebration of Rembrandt's birth in 2006. As the coordinating curator for the exhibition in Milwaukee, I am deeply grateful to both directors for their support in this important tribute to one of the greatest artists of all time.

My chief debt of thanks is to the lenders—institutions as well as private collectors—who graciously consented to part with their cherished works for almost five months. Every lender has been identified elsewhere in the exhibition and in publications, but I would like to single out Albertina Director Schröder for allowing 112 extraordinary works on paper to form the core of the exhibition. Lenders of paintings include the Princes Czartoryski Foundation in Cracow, who made available the famous *Landscape with the Good Samaritan*, one of only eight landscape paintings by Rembrandt; The Taft Museum in Cincinnati, The Minneapolis Institute of Arts, The J. Paul Getty Museum in Los Angeles, the Mauritshuis in The Hague, private collectors Mr. and Mrs. Frederick Vogel III, the Westerdijk private collection on long-term loan to the Milwaukee Art Museum, and a significant private collector of Dutch art who has lent seven works but wishes to remain anonymous.

The exhibition *Rembrandt and His Time* is accompanied by two separate but related publications. The first focuses on the masterworks from the Albertina and the second on the paintings that supplement the exhibition. For the first, I would like to offer my sincere thanks to Marian Bisanz-Prakken, curator of Netherlandish drawings at the Albertina, who helped shape the content of exhibition and who authored that catalogue. For the second book, I would like to acknowledge David de Witt, Bader Curator of Northern Baroque Art at Queens University, Ontario, and Mary Weaver Chapin, assistant curator of earlier European art at the Milwaukee Art Museum, for their entries in the catalogue. I would like to take this opportunity to offer a special note of appreciation for their contributions and scholarly expertise.

Colleagues in every department of the Milwaukee Art Museum have worked tirelessly to help bring this project to fruition. I am especially grateful to Catherine Sawinski, curatorial assistant, who helped with every aspect of the exhibition. Among the many others who provided assistance is Peggy MacArthur, grant director, who took on the daunting task of fundraising for the exhibition. Deeply appreciated are the efforts of Brigid Globensky, director of Education, who, with her staff, planned the innovative programming for the exhibition. My sincere thanks also go to Leigh Albritton, registrar, who dealt with the complex matters of insurance and shipping. For their help in many ways, it is a pleasure to also thank James DeYoung, Christine Davidian, Vicky Reddin, Larry Stadler, and John Irion.

For the beautiful books that accompany this exhibition, I am grateful to Steve Biel, book designer, whose sensitivity and clear-sightedness have produced two catalogues of exceptional elegance. I owe a very great debt to Terry Ann R. Neff of t.a. neff associates, inc., who guided the manuscript to completion with the assurance of a seasoned professional. She not only immeasurably improved the text, but her enthusiasm for the exhibition and the accompanying catalogues has sustained me throughout the project. Finally, to all who made this project possible, I extend my most sincere thanks.

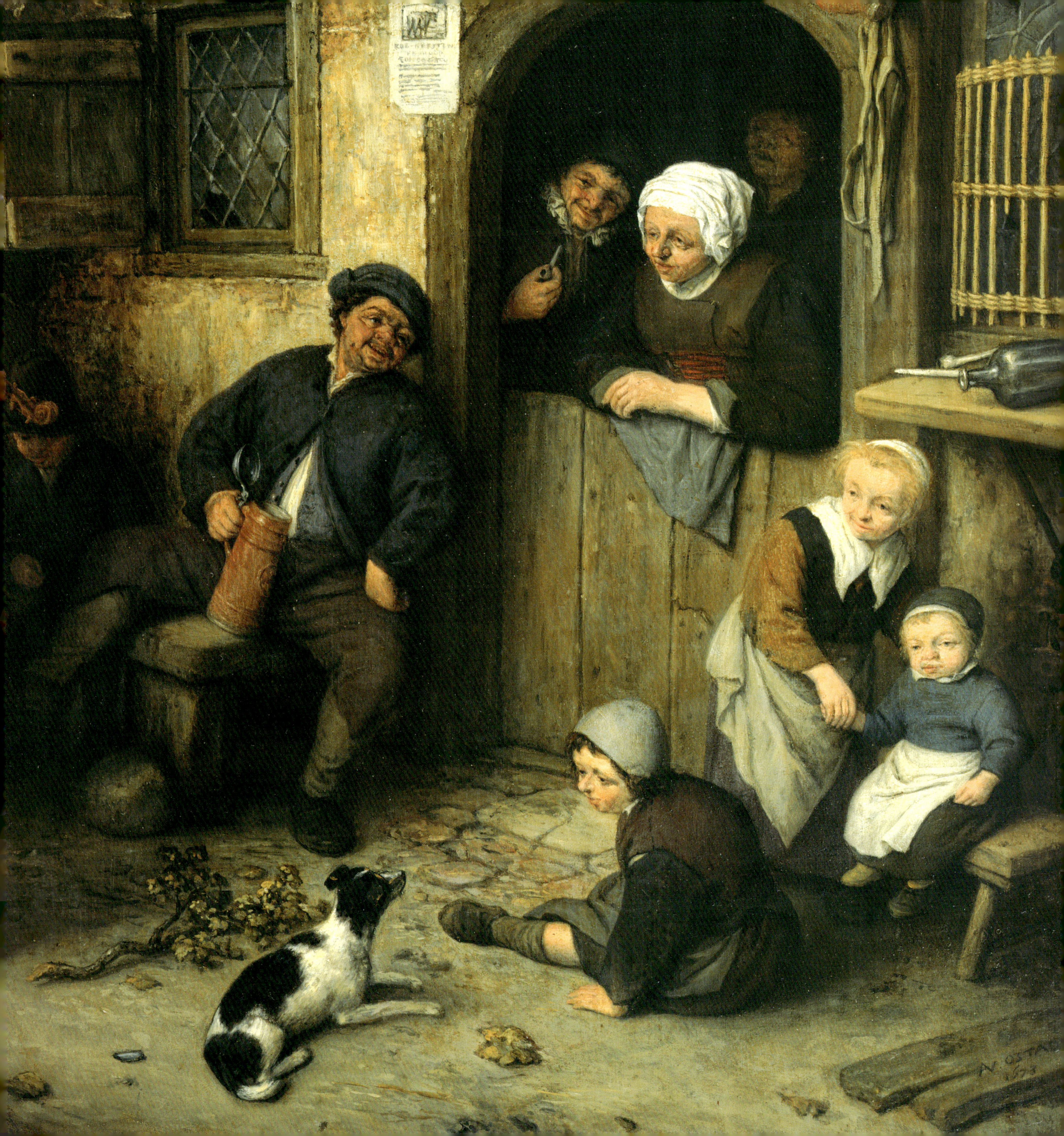

INTRODUCTION

LAURIE WINTERS

The fifteen paintings that supplement the exhibition *Rembrandt and His Time* demonstrate the range and achievement of seventeenth-century Netherlandish painting. With the independence of the United Provinces in 1609, Dutch art began making radical innovations, moving from its Mannerist and Flemish exemplars toward new forms and subjects. The Dutch delighted in naturalistic accounts of their surroundings, whether in the form of landscapes, portraits, still lifes, or genre paintings. In their desire to capture likenesses of their world, the Dutch created an art with an unprecedented truth to life.

Genre painting recording the character of middle-class daily life was one of the clearest expressions of naturalism in Holland. The spectrum ranged from depictions of industrious housewives and maidservants to renditions of the pleasures of the brothel, the free-wheeling country kermis, and taverns patronized by peasants. Yet for all this pictorial diversity, Dutch genre scenes always give the impression of a specific place and time.

The Dutch people's love of their homeland is nowhere clearer than in landscape painting. During the early 1600s, the Dutch reclaimed almost 200,000 acres from the inland seas, vastly increasing the size of their land. And in 1579, they gained a measure of independence from the Habsburg King of Spain. In this sense, their emphasis on landscape painting can be seen as a celebration of the unique characteristics of the lowlands and their economic prosperity. A group of Netherlandish artists working early in the seventeenth century laid the groundwork for a style increasingly based on the observation of nature. Bolder evocations followed, with expansive pictorial space and a low horizon that evoked the unified atmosphere and light of the Dutch countryside.

Panoramic vistas demonstrated the value of newly reclaimed and cultivated land. Even in Rembrandt's highly personal and romantic vision, the landscape is seen as a flat expanse carved with well-traveled roads and windmills in the distance. Succeeding landscape artists expanded not only the concept of the vista but its scale. Cities, the centers of Dutch commercial activity, were introduced into the backgrounds of paintings and new subjects emerged. The pride the Dutch felt in their newly won independence contributed to these new categories of subjects in painting.

Artists also took up the everyday themes of shipping on the rivers, canals, and the high sea. Scenes of fully loaded barges and fishermen at work remind the viewer that the waterways were as fundamental to Holland as the land itself. A key factor in the booming economic development of Holland, the sea was also the stage for naval battles. It was their greatest friend and sometimes their greatest foe—a necessary resource and a constant threat to both their land and their very lives. Maritime subjects reflected this dichotomy and ranged from merchant ships serenely at anchor or fishing vessels storm-tossed and threatened at sea.

Unusual or unexpected aspects of the land also appealed to the Dutch. Winter landscapes gained a new emphasis with many of the leading painters. While occasionally a time of suffering, winter offered a period of leisure and recreation for all levels of society, as is often reflected in scenes with skaters on frozen canals. By contrast, the Dutch Italianate landscape painters brought the endless sunshine of foreign lands to the Netherlands.

Whether depicting foreign lands, genre scenes, or even religious and mythological subjects, Dutch artists always emphasized the here and now in their selection of themes. Transcending mere topographical recordings of their world, the works of the Dutch Golden Age of art exemplify an enthusiastic affirmation of the artistic, social, and cultural values that can be called Dutch.

Jan van Goyen

Leiden 1596–1656 The Hague

1 *Landscape with Skaters,* 1643

2 *View of Nijmegen from the Northeast,* 1644

CAT. NO. 1

Oil on panel

39.5 x 51.1 cm

MONOGRAMMED AND INSCRIBED AT LOWER LEFT: "VG 1643"

Westerdijk Collection, Groningen, The Netherlands, currently on loan to the Milwaukee Art Museum L5.1993

PROVENANCE: Gooden & Fox, London, 1937/38; Asscher & Welker, London, 1938; P. de Boer, Amsterdam; Westerdijk Collection

BIBLIOGRAPHY: Beck 1973, G. 25

CAT. NO. 2

Oil on panel

38.5 x 52.1 cm

MONOGRAMMED AND INSCRIBED AT LOWER LEFT: "VG 1644"

Westerdijk Collection, Groningen, The Netherlands, currently on loan to the Milwaukee Art Museum L6.1993

PROVENANCE: Gooden & Fox, London, 1937/38; Asscher & Welker, London, 1938; P. de Boer, Amsterdam; Westerdijk Collection

BIBLIOGRAPHY: Beck 1973, G. 144

Jan van Goyen, one of the most important landscape painters of the Golden Age of Dutch art, was the son of a Leiden shoemaker. He began his career at the young age of ten, apprenticing with several local masters in Leiden before spending a year traveling in France. Upon his return, he moved to Haarlem around 1617 to work under Esaias van de Velde (1587–1630), one of the pioneers in the new mode of naturalistic landscape painting. Van Goyen's early work shows a great debt to this master.

Van Goyen returned to Leiden in 1618 and married Annetje Willemsdr van Raelst. The couple moved to The Hague, probably in the summer of 1632, where van Goyen would spend the greatest part of his career. Around this time, van Goyen, together with Salomon van Ruysdael (1600/3–1670) and Pieter de Molijn (1595–1661), developed a highly realistic approach to Dutch landscape painting known as tonalism. Using a restricted palette of browns, yellows, and ochers, these artists focused on creating softly luminous representations of the moist Dutch air, cool suffused light, and broad expanses of the flat landscape of Holland.

Although van Goyen spent most of his life in The Hague, he was an enthusiastic traveler and visited towns and cities across Holland, making sketches from life en route. The two paintings from the Westerdijk Collection, featuring the cities of Delft and Nijmegen, point to van Goyen's love of travel. Although not created as a pair, they are painted on oval panels of similar dimensions, a format van Goyen would use throughout his career. In addition, they function very well together as winter and summer views of Dutch cities.

In *Landscape with Skaters,* the artist depicted a typical winter scene in 1643. It is important to note that the weather in Holland was much colder in van Goyen's time than today. Much of the Northern Hemisphere experienced a drop in temperature, resulting in the so-called "Little Ice Age," which lasted from approximately 1350 to 1850. The cooler temperatures resulted in poor crops and a spread of disease, but some populations adapted and even prospered, taking to the ice for sport as well as transportation.

In this lively scene, the artist depicted a variety of villagers enjoying the outdoors. Van Goyen included all manner of charming detail to animate the scene. Adults, children, and even a skinny black

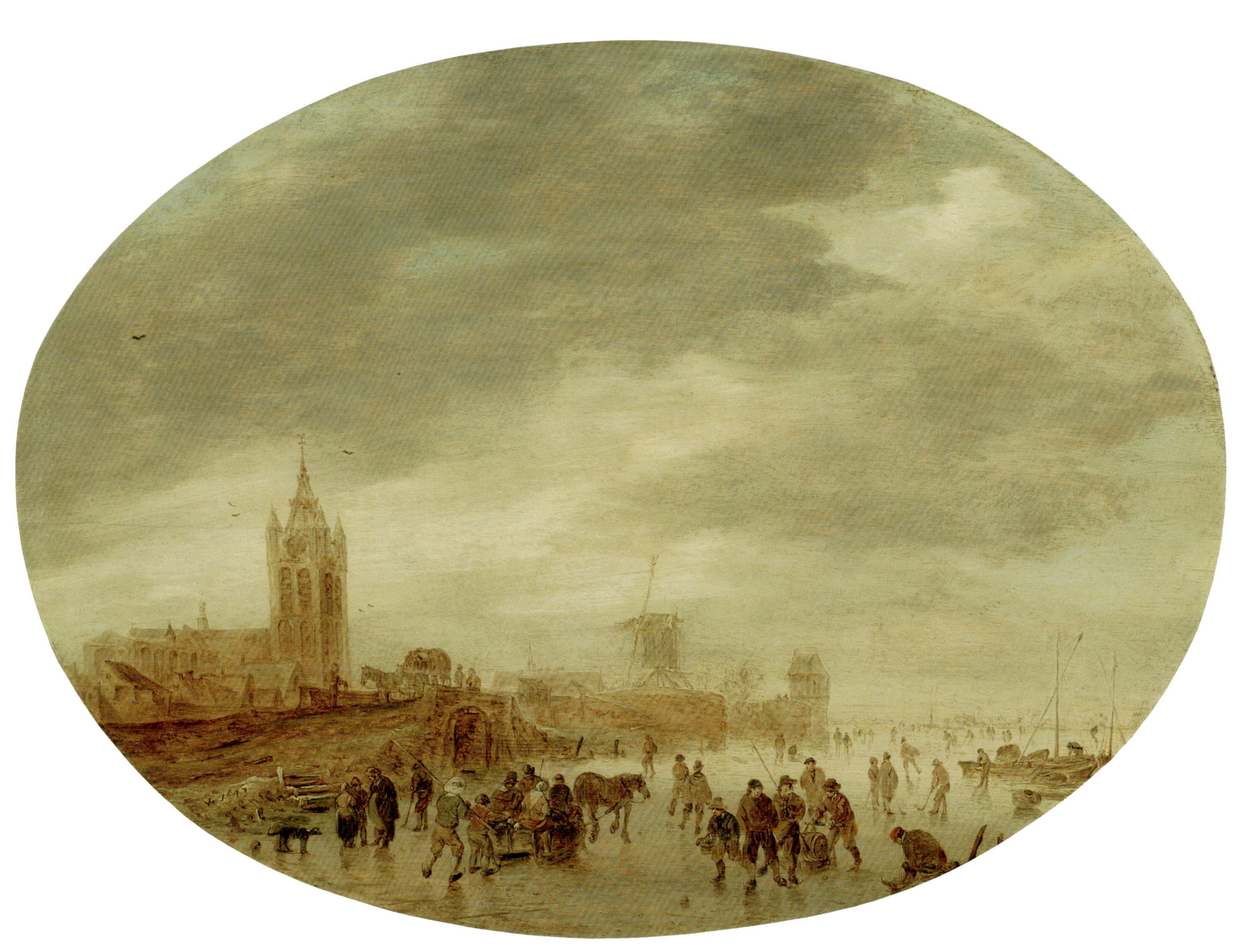

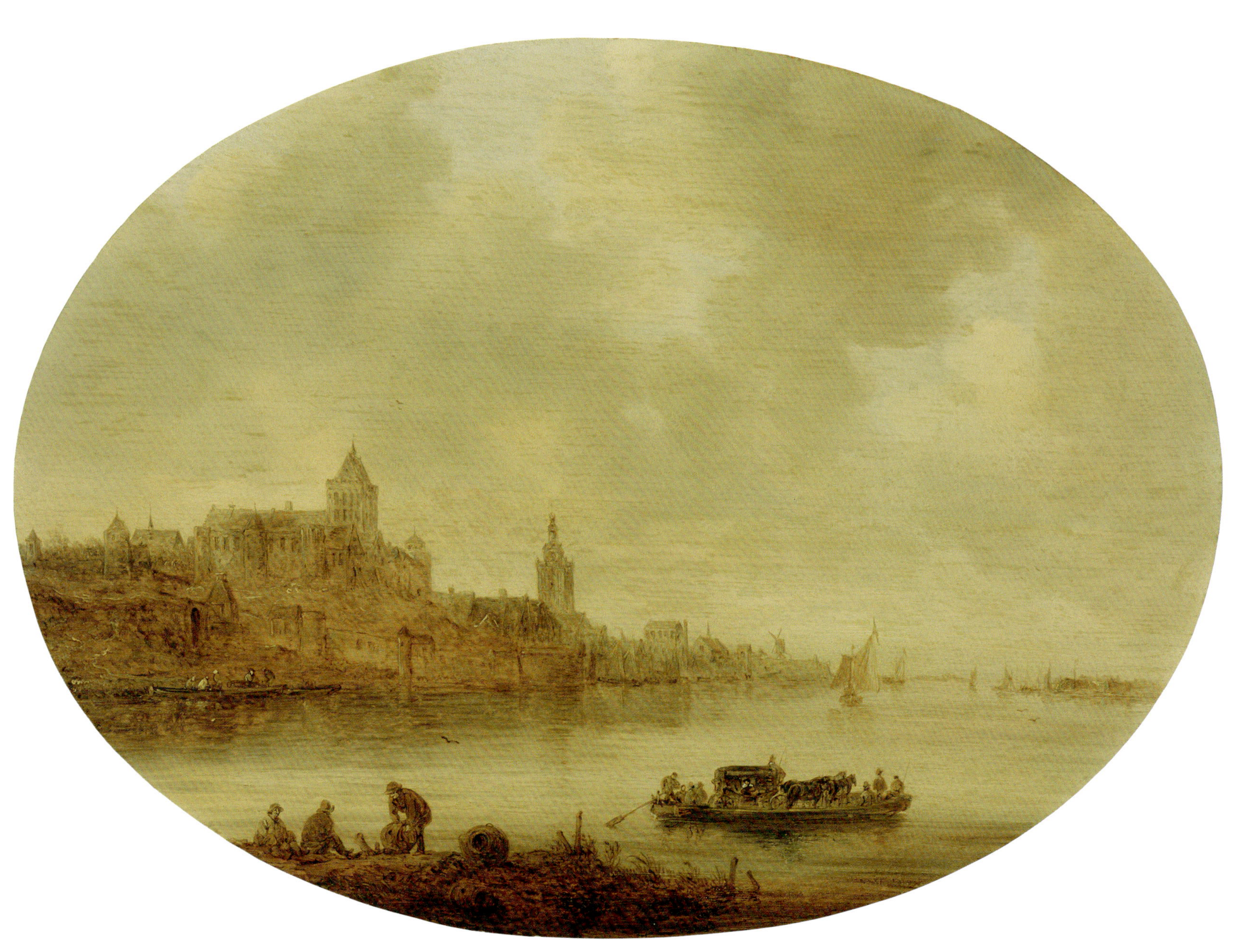

dog play and work on the icy canal. In the left foreground, a horse-drawn sled carries four people across the icy waterway as a young boy on skates holds onto the back of the sled to steal a ride. To the right, two men push a beer barrel on a sled toward the viewer, and a man with a bright red cap—one of the few touches of color in the painting—sits and laces up his skates. Behind him, two men and a boy play "kolf," a popular game related to hockey in which a ball is struck with a pole similar to a golf club or hockey stick.

Although the Dutch canals often froze completely, in this scene it appears that a few boats on the right bob in open water; several men stoop to unload the cargo, and van Goyen has very subtly suggested the line between the thick frozen ice (indeed, dense enough to support the weight of a horse and carriage) and the open water necessary for shipping. Behind the figures on the ice stretches the city of Delft, presided over by the Gothic Oude Kerk (Old Church). Its five distinctive spires tower above the old city center and the windmill to the right, adding a vertical thrust to this emphatically horizontal format.[1]

The palette of yellow, browns, and warm grays is characteristic of Goyen's paintings from the early and mid-1640s. As in many of his panoramic landscapes, however, it is the sky, rather than the land or the water, that covers most of the panel. A master at evoking the complex, changing Dutch light, here van Goyen captured the shifting clouds and small patches of pale blue sky. The rosy undersides of the clouds suffuse the scene with a warm glow. The contrast of dark and lighter areas further animates the cloudy expanse. Van Goyen used a low horizon line to suggest the endlessness of the Dutch landscape and give even greater emphasis to the atmospheric conditions above.

In van Goyen's view of Nijmegen of the following year, the artist turned his attention to a summer scene. Nijmegen, located in the province of Gelderland near the modern border with Germany, was a frequent subject for the artist in the years 1633–54. The oldest city in Holland, Nijmegen was blessed with picturesque details that appealed to artists, including ancient fortifications, the fine Renaissance Grote Kerk (Great Church), and the scenic Waal River. In this landscape, van Goyen approached the city from the northeast, creating such a distinctive view that even today it is possible to identify this site.

As with the winter scene of Delft, the sky dominates the picture. The three men in the foreground help establish scale, yet the perspective is slightly skewed; the figures and horse-drawn carriage on the barge behind the men are strangely dwarfed, appearing miniscule in comparison to the foreground figures. Behind the barge, numerous sailboats ply the river; van Goyen seems to have been particularly fond of sailboats, which appear prominently in his painting by the 1640s.

The style is understated. Closely related ochers, browns, and silvery grays create a unifying tonal atmosphere. Van Goyen subtly indicated the shadow cast by the city onto the placid surface of the Waal River. The few sparing touches of white paint draw the viewer's eye to the left edge of the composition, where five figures appear to embark in two low barges.

Van Goyen was highly regarded during his lifetime. He was named "hoofdman" ("headman") of The Hague painters guild in 1638 and 1640. In 1651, several years after these two panels were painted, the municipality commissioned him to paint a large panoramic view of the town for the Burgomaster's room in the Town Hall. He was also an influential teacher, tutoring his son-in-law, Jan Steen (1626–1679) as well as Nicolaes Berchem (1620–1683) and Adriaen van der Cabel (1630/31–1705). His influence can be found in the work of numerous artists, including the early paintings of Aelbert Cuyp (1620–1691).[2]

Van Goyen was not only a prolific painter and draftsman, but also worked as an art appraiser, auctioneer, and real estate and tulip speculator. His unsuccessful ventures in the tulip market crippled his finances, and at the time of his death in 1656, his entire estate was sold to satisfy his debts. MWC

1 I thank David de Witt for identifying the city. See the related drawing *The Oude Kerk at Delft in Fantasy Setting*, 1640–45, in the Kupferstichkabinett, Staatliche Museen, Berlin.

2 On van Goyen's influence, see Beck, 1991.

Jan van Goyen

Leiden 1596–1656 The Hague

3 *View of Duurstede Castle,* 1649

Oil on panel

52.7 x 73.7 cm

The J. Paul Getty Museum, Los Angeles

PROVENANCE: Mme. Gaudry, Paris, by inheritance, c. 1800; Eugene
Slatter Gallery, London, by 1954; D. G. Stirling sale, Sotheby's
London, June 24, 1959, lot 62; J. Paul Getty, Malibu and Sutton Place,
Surrey, 1959–76; estate of J. Paul Getty, 1976–78; distributed to
The J. Paul Getty Museum, Los Angeles, 1978

BIBLIOGRAPHY: *ARTnews* 1954; Beck 1973, no. 697; Sutton 1986, p. 144

Jan van Goyen's many walking trips through the Dutch countryside
provided him opportunities to sketch the picturesque towns, cities, and
ancient castles that dotted the flat land. He used his drawings as the
basis for oil paintings created in his studio. He painted the imposing
castle at Wijk bij Duurstede (a town on the lower Rhine southeast of
Utrecht) a number of times. This example is from 1649.[1] Built around
700 A.D., the castle originated as a military fortification with thick walls
and tall towers to repel invading Vikings. It was pillaged around 850,
but subsequently rebuilt and embellished over the years.[2] By van Goyen's
time, it had became a magnificent conglomeration of residential wings,
courtyards, and turrets, including the striking round Burgundian
tower at the far right of this present composition.

The viewer enters this luminous painting by means of the
activity in the foreground. A horse-drawn coach and several passengers
cross the river in a slow-moving ferry; at the left, three fisherman
prepare to haul in their nets. Two cows on the far right add a bucolic
touch. Although the water is perfectly smooth and reflective, van Goyen
suggested wind by the taut sails of the boats on the left, and especially
by the dramatic, cloud-covered sky.

As in van Goyen's best works, the atmosphere plays a central role.
The very low horizon line allows the sky to dominate two-thirds of the
panel. The foreground of the painting exhibits a slightly darker palette,
as the bluish cloud in the upper left corner temporarily blocks the sun,
while the castle, carefully rendered in pale blue, green, and gray, appears
to shimmer. Toward the end of his career, van Goyen expanded his color
range beyond the monochromatic "tonal" phase he began in the 1630s.
Nonetheless, his palette remained restricted in the over twelve hundred
known paintings he produced in his fifty-year career.

Although he often began by working from life, van Goyen
freely altered the proportions of buildings, the curve of a river, or the
placement of a tree to create the desired effect.[3] More than mere
topographical recordings, the landscapes are sensitive and artful interpretations of the shifting light, atmosphere, and conditions of his
homeland. His contemporaries valued these "landscape portraits" of their
country; it is even possible that these paintings had a patriotic function
as well.[4] Not only had the Dutch recently reclaimed approximately
200,000 acres from the inland seas during the early 1600s, vastly
increasing the size of their land, but since 1579, they were also enjoying
new political independence from the Habsburg King of Spain, Philip II.
In this sense, the celebration of the distinctive, flat, watery landscape
can be seen as a reflection of national awareness and pride. MWC

1 For other views of Duurstede Castle, see Beck 1973, vol. 2, nos. 414, 637. Jacob van Ruisdael's
famous painting *The Mill*, Rijksmuseum, Amsterdam, also features the castle.

2 *Duits Quarterly* 1 (1963), pp. 11–13.

3 On van Goyen's artistic liberties, see C. J. de Bruyn Kops in Amsterdam/Boston/Philadelphia
1987–88, p. 328.

4 See S. Schama, "Dutch Landscapes: Culture as Foreground," in ibid., pp. 64–83.

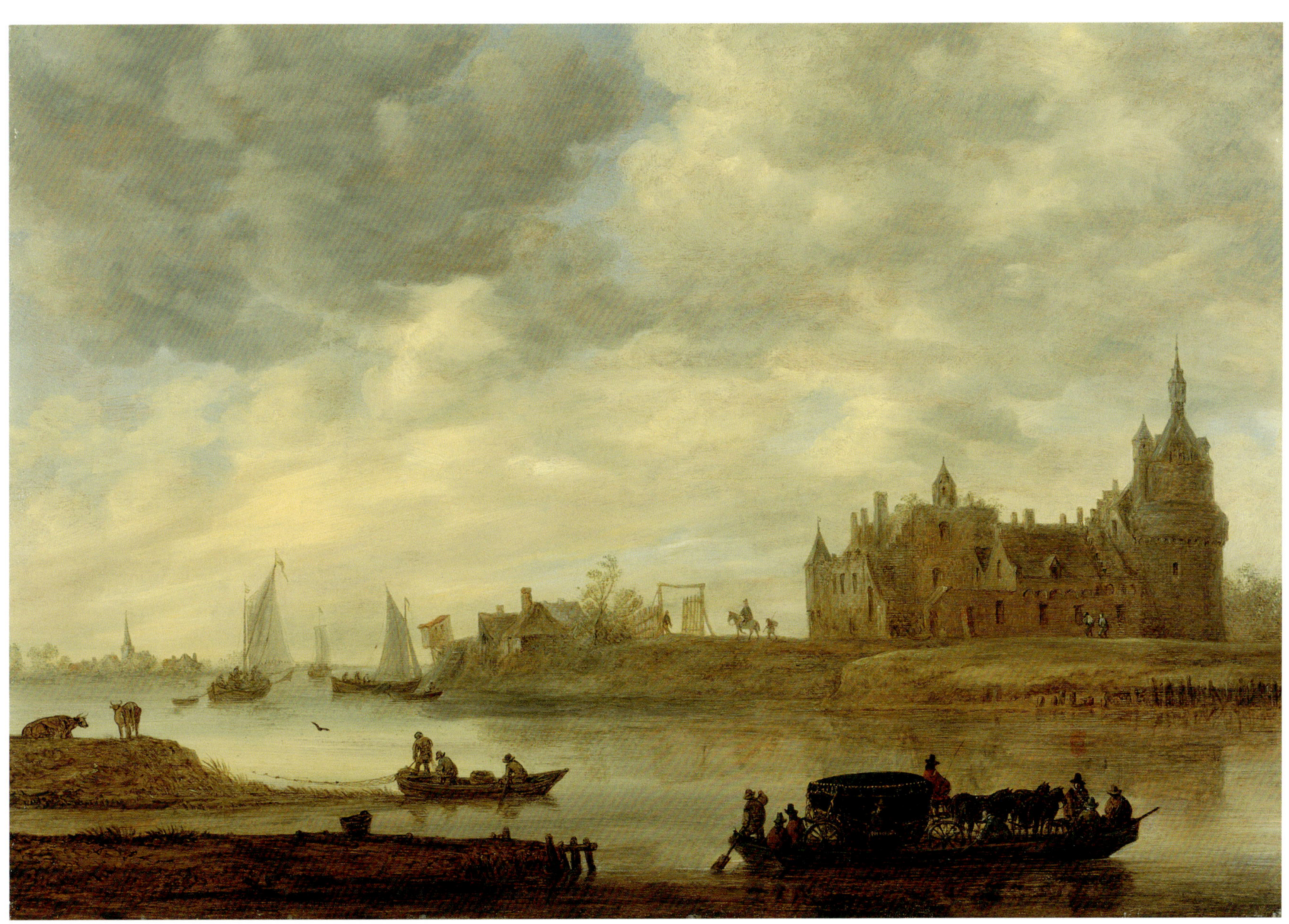

Rembrandt Harmensz. van Rijn

LEIDEN 1606–1669 AMSTERDAM

4 *Landscape with the Good Samaritan,* 1638

INSCRIBED AT LOWER RIGHT: "Rembrandt f. 1638"

Oil on panel

46.5 x 66 cm

The Princes Czartoryski Museum, Cracow (inv. no. 105)

PROVENANCE: M.D. Eversdijk, sale, The Hague, May 18, 1766, no. 75; Vassal de Saint-Hubert, sale, Paris, Jan. 17, 1774, no. 22; Jean-Pierre Norblin, Paris and Cracow; A. J. Czartoryski, Cracow, by c. 1813; The Princes Czartoryski Museum, Cracow

BIBLIOGRAPHY: For an extensive early bibliography, see *Corpus* 1982– (Rembrandt Research Project), vol. 3, pp. 265–270, A125; Schneider 1990, pp. 122–27, 178–81, no. 4, illus; and Cracow 2001, p. 80, illus.

Rembrandt Harmensz. van Rijn was born in Leiden in 1606, the eighth of at least ten children of the prosperous miller Harmen Gerritsz. van Rijn and his wife, Neeltgen van Zuybrouck.[1] The family mill stood on the banks of the Rhine River, hence his surname van Rijn ("of the Rhine"). Rembrandt attended the Leiden Latin School and in 1620 went to the University of Leiden, but soon left to study painting with the Leiden artist Jacob Isaacz. van Swanenburgh (1571–1638). After three years, Rembrandt left in 1624 for Amsterdam, where he studied with the leading history painter Pieter Lastman (1583–1633).

By 1625, Rembrandt was back in Leiden, where he quickly developed a reputation as a portraitist and history painter. His fame spread rapidly, and by 1631 he had met the Amsterdam art dealer Hendrik van Uylenburgh (c. 1587–1661) and was painting the likenesses of well-to-do Amsterdam families. Around 1632, Rembrandt seemingly moved to Amsterdam, where he ran van Uylenburgh's studio until 1635. He achieved tremendous success, receiving many commissions and attracting numerous students.

In 1634, he married van Uylenburg's niece, Saskia van Uylenburg (1612–1642), daughter of a prominent burgomaster from Friesland. In 1639, at the height of his success, he purchased the large house in Amsterdam that he would occupy for fifteen years. To do so, he borrowed heavily, incurring a debt that would contribute to his financial difficulties in the mid-1650s. After a long illness, Saskia died in 1642, before the age of thirty. Titus was the only one of their four children to survive infancy.[2]

Titus's nurse Geertje Dirckx became a companion to Rembrandt until he dismissed her in 1649 and entered a lifelong relationship with Hendrickje Stoffels. The two never married, but in 1654 they had a daughter, Cornelia. Beset by financial problems, Rembrandt declared insolvency in 1656; in 1657 and 1658, his estate, including his large art collection, was auctioned to pay his debts.[3] Despite numerous important portrait commissions during the late 1650s and early 1660s, his deeply personal manner of painting became less fashionable. Although he remained famous, he became isolated from the mainstreams of Dutch art and never regained financial solvency. Hendrickje and Titus both died before him. When Rembrandt did die in 1669, he was buried in an unknown rented grave in the Westerkerk, Amsterdam.

Landscape with the Good Samaritan is an extremely rare landscape painting from the late 1630s. Landscapes make up a relatively small percentage of Rembrandt's oeuvre. In 1836, John Smith, the first cataloguer of his paintings, recorded only nineteen landscapes, all done between the mid-1630s and the mid-1640s. Cynthia P. Schneider, today's foremost scholar on Rembrandt's landscapes, gives only eight of those to the artist with certainty; the attribution of the other eleven is hotly debated.[4]

Rembrandt first introduced landscape into his paintings in the mid-1620s as a background for his historical subjects. Combining

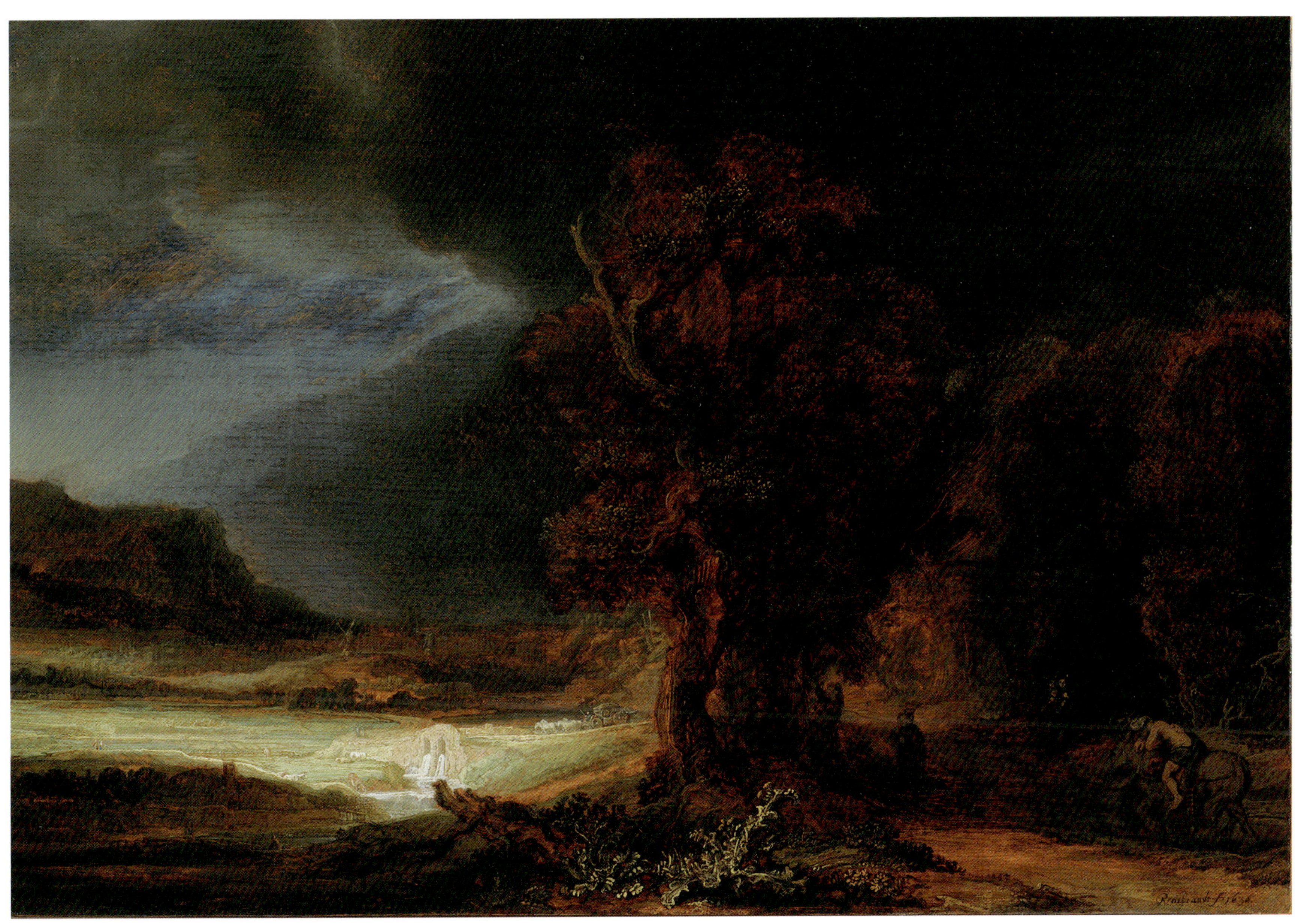

Rembrandt f. 1638

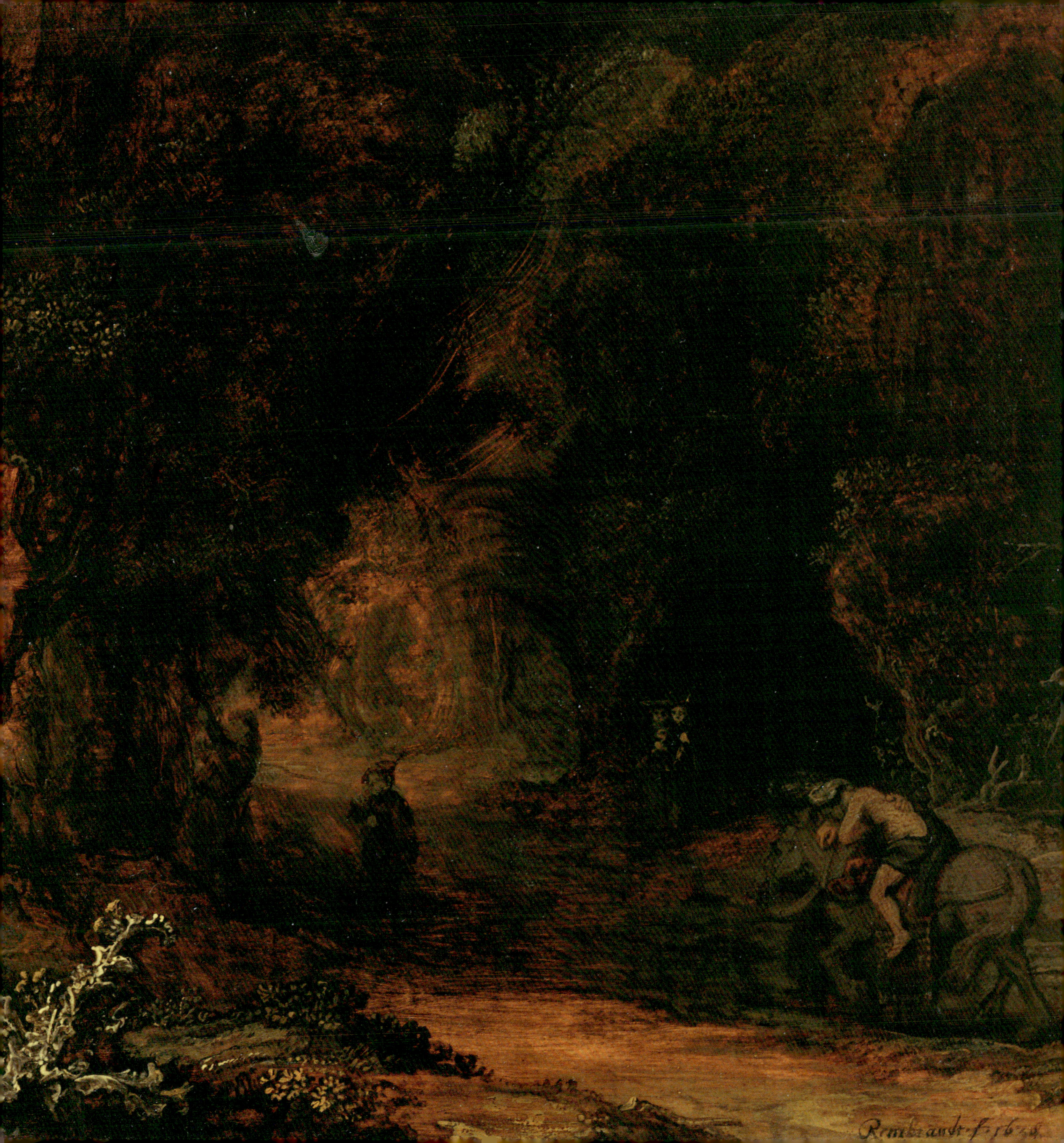
Rembrandt f 1638

realistic and imaginary motifs, he created settings that enhanced the drama of the narrative. Gradually the landscape assumed a greater dominance in helping to tell the story, ultimately encompassing highly charged metaphorical references. In this evolution, Rembrandt was likely influenced by the fantastic landscapes of Hercules Seghers (1589/90–1633/38), whose work he admired.[5] Rembrandt's scenes, however, are transitions from the fantastic to the romantic. Contrasts of light and dark, soft and harmonious colors, lively thick paint surfaces, and often the threat of an impending storm heighten the drama. The composition of these small landscapes is often unified by views through arches and by bridges and roads traversed by small figures making their way across the land.

Landscape with the Good Samaritan depicts a rare moment in the famous parable (Luke 10: 34) that allowed Rembrandt to concentrate on the landscape. It tells the story of a traveler who was attacked by robbers and left for dead. A priest and a Levite both passed the wounded man but only the Samaritan—a traditional enemy of the Jews—conveyed him to an inn where he could receive proper care. The story evidently interested Rembrandt, who made at least seven drawings and one etching of the subject.[6] Only the painting concentrates on the journey to the inn, whereby Rembrandt could focus on nature itself to carry meaning.

The panoramic late sixteenth-century model forms the core of Rembrandt's design. Seghers's influence is seen in the dark profile of the craggy mountains of the background, the broad plain animated by numerous details, and the central motif in the foreground. However, Rembrandt transformed the Mannerist formula with naturalistic details such as farmhouses, windmills, and grazing cattle, creating a dramatic juxtaposition of the everyday and the imaginary. The two gnarled, entwined trees—one flourishing and the other nearly bare—are likewise derived from an earlier artist, Hendrick Goltzius (1558–1617), and may be a metaphor for the wounded man and the Samaritan, bound together by an act of kindness.[7] The trees also serve as a compositional fulcrum for the figures moving throughout the landscape.

The diminutive size of the figures relative to the landscape underscores the isolated action of the Good Samaritan within a vast and threatening world. Two tiny figures, possibly the priest and the Levite, walk down the road in the distance beyond the bridge. The wounded man is near the right edge, half-naked and slumped over the beast that transports him. The Samaritan, on the path before him, stops to watch a hunter shooting into a tree, possibly reinforcing the notion of the value of action.[8] Behind the hunter is an elegantly dressed couple who may represent idle luxury, in contrast to the selfless behavior of the Samaritan. Rembrandt used these familiar motifs as a means of emphasizing the contemporary relevance of the biblical story. LW

1 For biographical background on Rembrandt, refer to classic texts like Hofstede de Groot 1907–27, vol. 6; Rosenberg 1948; Slive 1953; and more recently, White 1984.

2 White 1984. Rembrandt's purchase in 1639 of the large house on the edge of the country and Saskia's death in 1642 are often seen as catalysts to his interest in landscape.

3 Wheelock 1995, pp. 204–205.

4 Schneider 1990, pp. 1–2. Cynthia P. Schneider's seminal publication on Rembrandt's landscapes provides not only a summary of previous interpretations but a thoughtful integration of new ideas. This entry relies heavily on her work.

5 Ibid., pp. 122–23.

6 Ibid., pp. 178–81.

7 Ibid., pp. 123–24.

8 Ibid., p. 180.

Rembrandt Harmensz. van Rijn, attributed to

LEIDEN 1606–1669 AMSTERDAM

5 *Head of a Bearded Man: Study for St. Matthew,* c. 1661

Oil on wood

24.5 x 19.7 cm

Private Collection

PROVENANCE: Paul Mathey, Paris; Kleinberger, Paris; Ludwig Mandl, Wiesbaden; C. A. Mandl, Hamburg; Sale, Frederik Muller, Amsterdam, July 19, 1923, lot 127, illus.; E. Nicholas, Paris; Sir Harold Samuel, London; Private Collection, England; sale, Christie's, London, Feb. 24, 1995, lot 96, illus.; Private Collection

BIBLIOGRAPHY: Hofstede de Groot 1908–27, vol. 6, p. 123, no. 175 (as Rembrandt); Hofstede de Groot 1912, pp. 182, 188; Valentiner 1923, p. xxviii, no. 105, p. 99, illus.; Rosenberg 1948, pp. 106, 112, fig. 99; Bauch 1966, p. 13, no. 233, illus.; Rosenberg, Slive, and Ter Kuile 1966, p. 78; Regteren Altena 1967, pp. 70–71; Gerson 1968, p. 436, fig. 387, p. 503, no. 387 (as Rembrandt, enlarged on all four sides); Bredius and Gerson 1969, p. 573, no. 304, illus. (as Rembrandt); Berlin/ Amsterdam/London 1991–92, p. 267, with no. 47; Wheelock 1995, pp. 333, 334 no. 6; Melbourne 1997, p. 162; Slive 1998, p. 182, no. 182; Washington/Los Angeles 2005, pp. 95, 134, no. 3

This small painting depicts the head of a man in robust middle age, with a heavy, thick beard, prominent brow and cheekbones, and pronounced muscles flanking the nose. He turns to the right and looks off to the side. His lowered eyelids, furrowed brow, pursed lips, and open gaze suggest that he is absorbed in thought. His expression and features connect him directly to Rembrandt's well-known 1661 *St. Matthew Inspired by the Angel* in the Louvre.[1] However, the Paris work does not appear to be the source for this painting. There, the apostle is seen more on a level, and draws his hand to his chin. He wears a turbanlike headdress, not the soft cap and heavy smock seen here. The differences between the two may reflect the transformation of a life study from a model into a finished biblical painting. The simple costume in the small panel is derived from contemporary dress, bereft of any historical allusions. It seems highly likely that the present work reflects Rembrandt's study of a figure in preparation for the St. Matthew. The question remains whether it is an original sketch by Rembrandt or a copy after one. Depictions by him of Jeremiah and of Jesus seem to have been preceded in a similar fashion by less formal, but finished, paintings of heads.[2]

Bredius identifies this panel as autograph, and groups it with three other small panels showing the same model in slightly varying views.[3] However, none of these other works approaches its decisive handling and structure. The example in Washington is an exercise in direct impasto strokes, but its overall impression is not strong. Here, by contrast, the thick strokes collaborate throughout to evoke solid form, in the highlight on the cap, the bridge of the nose, and in the mesmerizing wrinkled forehead. In several remarkably deft passages in the beard and hair, impasto strokes serve to highlight the form and texture instead of creating a decorative surface pattern. Also significant is the solidity of the facial contours on the shadow side—an aspect critical to defining form but almost always neglected by Rembrandt's followers. Additionally, in its technical range, the panel displays in the rendering of the smock some smooth and broad strokes in thin sensuous layers—Rembrandt's hallmark during this period. Furthermore, it is the only panel among the four that leaves space around the head (misinterpreted by Hofstede de Groot and Gerson as the result of additions), thereby anticipating a finished composition.

In 1968, Horst Gerson singled out this panel among the group of four study heads related to the *St. Matthew* as the only one likely by Rembrandt.[4] The question of definitive authorship revolves around

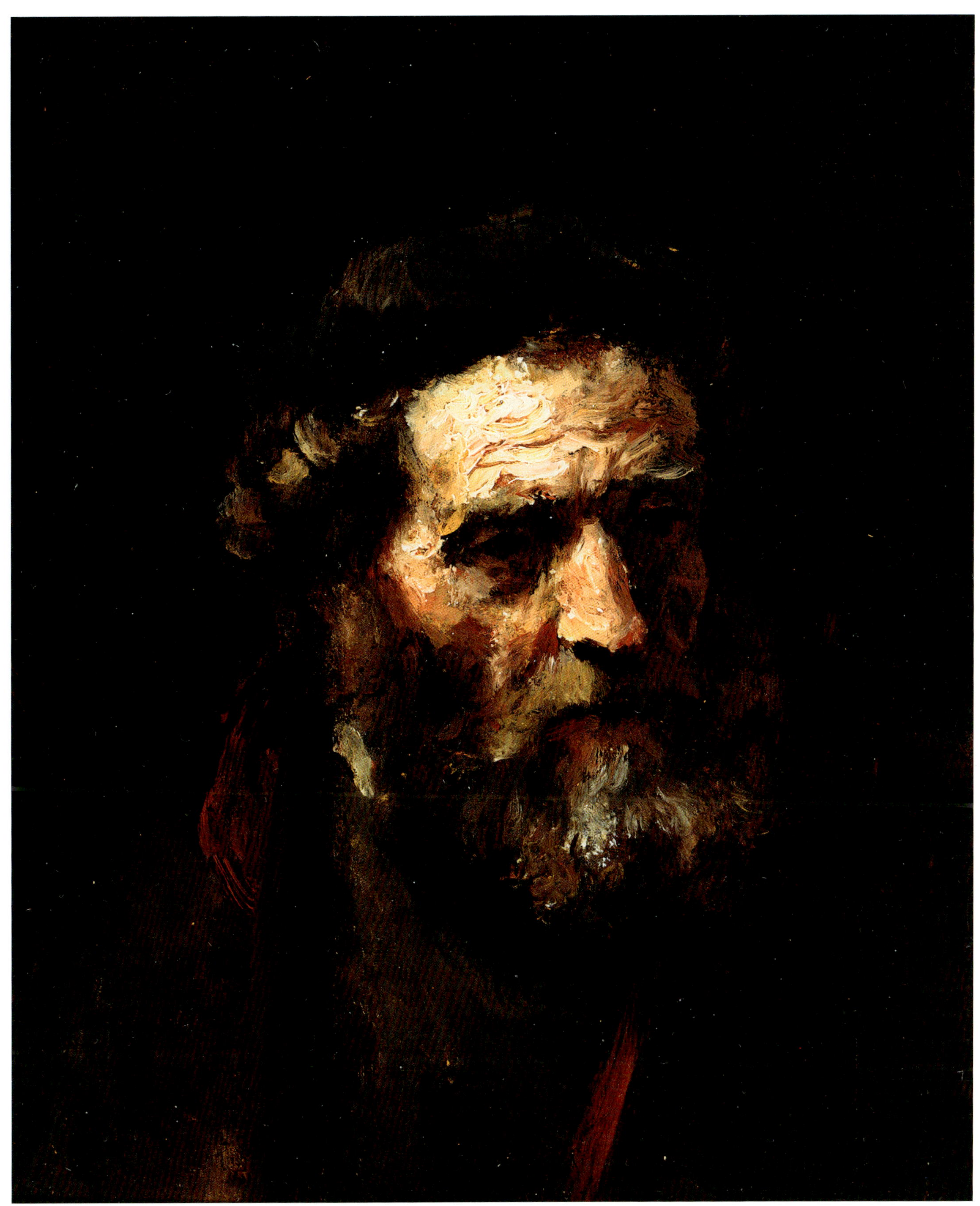

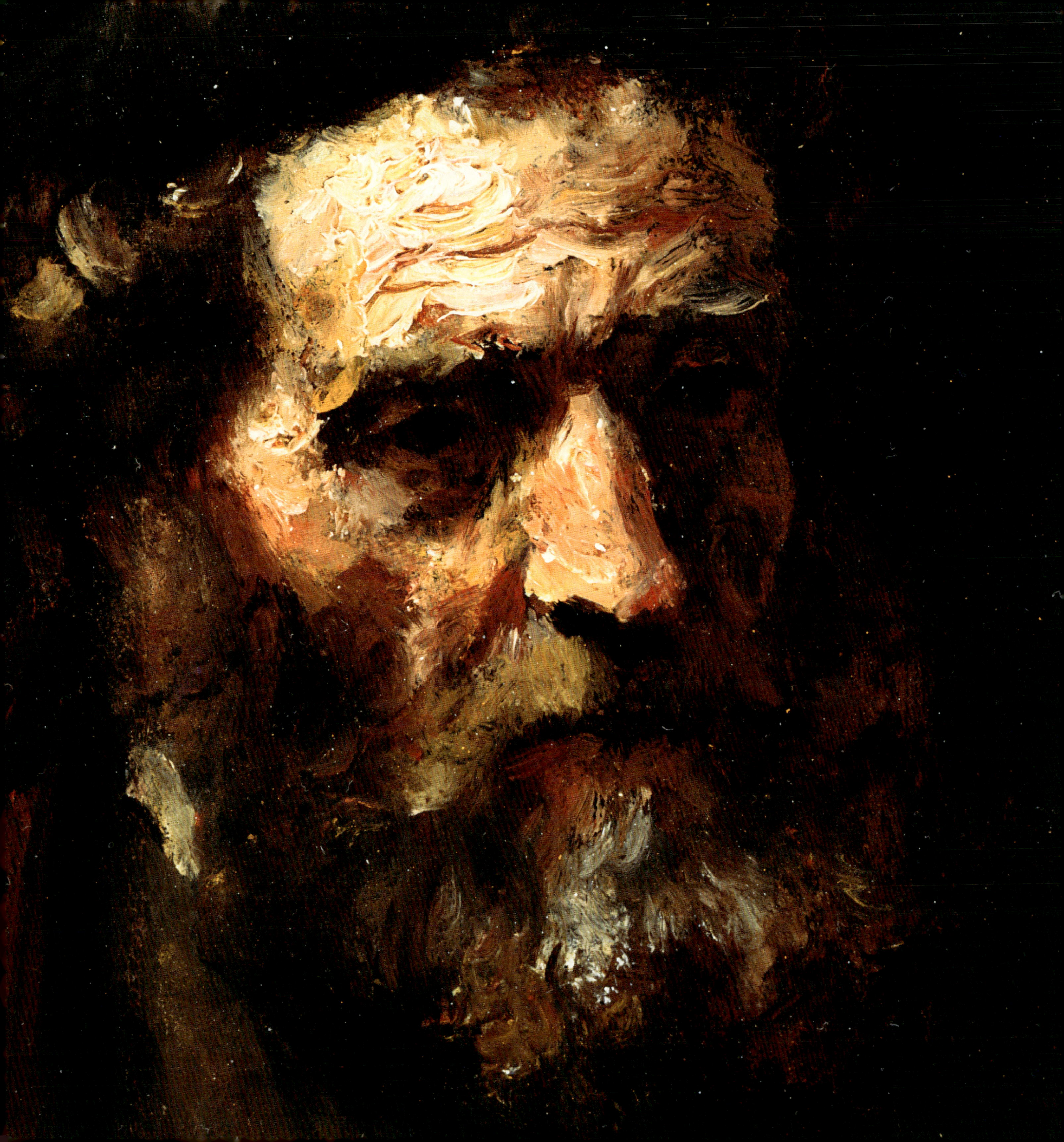

a significant lacuna in our knowledge of the master: it is not known
whether Rembrandt made preparatory painted sketches in a manner
possibly even looser than the rough style in his finished paintings. It has
been recognized that around 1658, he made a painted sketch for his
printed portrait of Lieven Willemsz. van Coppenol.[5]

An important precedent for the present work appears to have
been a painting from around 1657 in The National Gallery, London,
connected by scholars to a finished *Man in Fantasy Costume* in the
Hermitage, St. Petersburg.[6] Intriguingly, the London painting is similar
to the present picture in the figure's type and pose, as well as its
compositional placement in a larger, empty space. However, the man's
features differ, and the smoother, more finished technique is closer
to Rembrandt's finished paintings of the late 1650s. In the present
work, the handling is rougher than is typical even for the master's
latest period, and could find explanation only in the function of a
preparatory sketch. DDW

1 *Matthew and the Angel*, oil on canvas, 96 x 81 cm, Paris, Musée du Louvre, inv. no. 1738.
  See Bredius and Gerson 1969, p. 613, no. 614, illus.

2 Rembrandt produced in various media a large number of depictions of the model used in
  his c. 1631 painting *Jeremiah Lamenting the Destruction of Jerusalem* in the Rijksmuseum,
  Amsterdam. The most prominent is *Head of an Old Man in a Cap*, oil on wood, 24.3 x 20.3 cm,
  signed, Kingston, Agnes Etherington Art Centre, acc. no. 46-031. See Kingston 2003;
  Kassel/Amsterdam 2001–2002, pp. 370–73, no. 80, illus. Bredius lists several similar small
  related depictions of Jesus. See Bredius and Gerson 1969, p. 614, nos. 620–27, illus. Of these,
  the Philadelphia and Berlin examples are the only ones likely by Rembrandt. They appear
  to have served as studies for *Jesus*, oil on canvas, 108 x 89 cm, Glens Falls, New York, Hyde
  Collection. See ibid., p. 614, no. 628, illus.

3 Oil on wood, 25 x 22 cm, Bayonne, Musée Bonnat, inv. no. 972. See ibid., p. 573, no. 303,
  illus. Oil on wood, 27 x 22 cm, Detroit, Collection of William J. McAneeny. See ibid., p. 573,
  no. 305, illus. Oil on wood, 25 x 19.5 cm, Washington, D. C., National Gallery of Art
  (Widener Collection). See ibid., p. 573, no. 302, illus.

4 Ibid., p. 573.

5 Oil on wood, 36.6 x 28.9 cm, New York, The Metropolitan Museum of Art. See ibid., p. 572,
  no. 291, illus. See Ronni Baer, "Rembrandt's Oil Sketches," in Boston/Chicago 2003–2004,
  p. 38, illus.

6 *A Bearded Man in a Cap*, oil on canvas, 78 x 66.5 cm, signed "Rembrandt f. 165.," London,
  The National Gallery. See Bredius and Gerson 1969, p. 571, no. 283, illus.; *Man in Fantasy
  Costume*, oil on canvas, 71 x 61 cm, indistinctly signed "Rembrandt f.1661," St. Petersburg,
  State Hermitage Museum. See ibid., p. 573, no. 309, illus.

Adriaen van Ostade

Haarlem 1610–1685 Haarlem

6 *Interior of an Inn with Three Men and a Boy,* 1656

Oil on panel

33.8 x 39.5 cm

Inscribed at lower left: "Av ostade 1656"

The Taft Museum, Cincinnati

Provenance: Comte d'Orsay, sale, Paris, Mar. 20, 1810; Jean-Louis Laneuville, portraitist and pupil of David, sale, Paris, Nov. 6 et. seq., 1811; John Smith, 1825; William Beckford, 1829; Colonel de Biré, sale, M. Héris, Brussels, Paris, Mar. 25–26, 1841, no. 48; Thomas Agnew and Sons, London, 1905; Taft Collection, purchased through Scott and Fowles, New York, Sept. 30, 1905; The Taft Museum, Cincinnati

Bibliography: Smith 1829, vol.1, pp. 147–48, no. 145; Hofstede de Groot 1907–28, vol. 3, p. 263, no. 414f; Mireur 1911, vol. 5, p. 28, under 1811, Laneuville; Brockwell 1920, no. 18; Sullivan 1995, pp. 147–49, illus.

Adriaen van Ostade is one of the undisputed masters of rustic genre scenes in seventeenth-century Holland. Houbraken describes van Ostade and Adriaen Brouwer as pupils of Frans Hals at the same time, with Brouwer a significant influence on van Ostade's early subject matter.[1] Van Ostade's career was pursued entirely in Haarlem, where he served as "hoofdman" ("headman") of the painters guild in 1647 and 1661, and dean in 1662.[2] A prolific artist, his known works number more than eight hundred paintings, about fifty etchings, and some four hundred drawings and watercolors. His successful career inspired many imitators and included several gifted pupils: his brother Isack van Ostade (1621–1649), Cornelis Bega (1631–1664), Cornelis Dusart (1660–1704), and possibly Jan Steen (1625/26–1679).

With its focus on peasant figures within a softly illuminated interior and its beautifully harmonized colors, *Interior of an Inn with Three Men and a Boy* is characteristic of the artist's mature work. The modest setting has long mistakenly been interpreted as "a carpenter's shop" because the man near the window holds a wooden panel and the generations of men at the left suggest a kind of family apprenticeship.[3] In 1995, Walter A. Liedtke proposed an alternative reading of the scene.[4] The chalkboard on the back wall and the wooden shoe (presumably used as a chalk holder) nailed next to it were commonly used in taverns of the period to record the drinks consumed by customers. A man in the left corner can be seen offering a reluctant young boy a glass of beer. According to Liedtke, this interior is likely "the main room of a modest dwelling that, as part of a common cottage industry, also functions as a local pub."[5]

Signs of domesticity in the dilapidated cottage have been relegated to a secondary role. A yarn winder hangs from the ceiling; an earthenware cooking pot sits on the floor; a sewing basket with a hand winder and a distaff rest next to an empty basket on a broken bench. This is not the well-run domestic setting found in so many Dutch pictures. The moralizing lesson of a household turned upside down by the ill effects of alcohol is perhaps signaled by the scruffy dog in the center that looks out toward the viewer as if patiently awaiting the return of its master and perhaps a return to order. LW

1 Sullivan 1995, p. 147; Slive 1995, pp. 135–36. For dates pertaining to van Ostade's life and work, see Schnackenburg 1981, vol. 1, pp. 13–16.

2 Schnackenburg 1981, vol. 1, pp. 13–16.

3 Sullivan 1995, p. 148.

4 Ibid., p. 147.

5 Ibid.

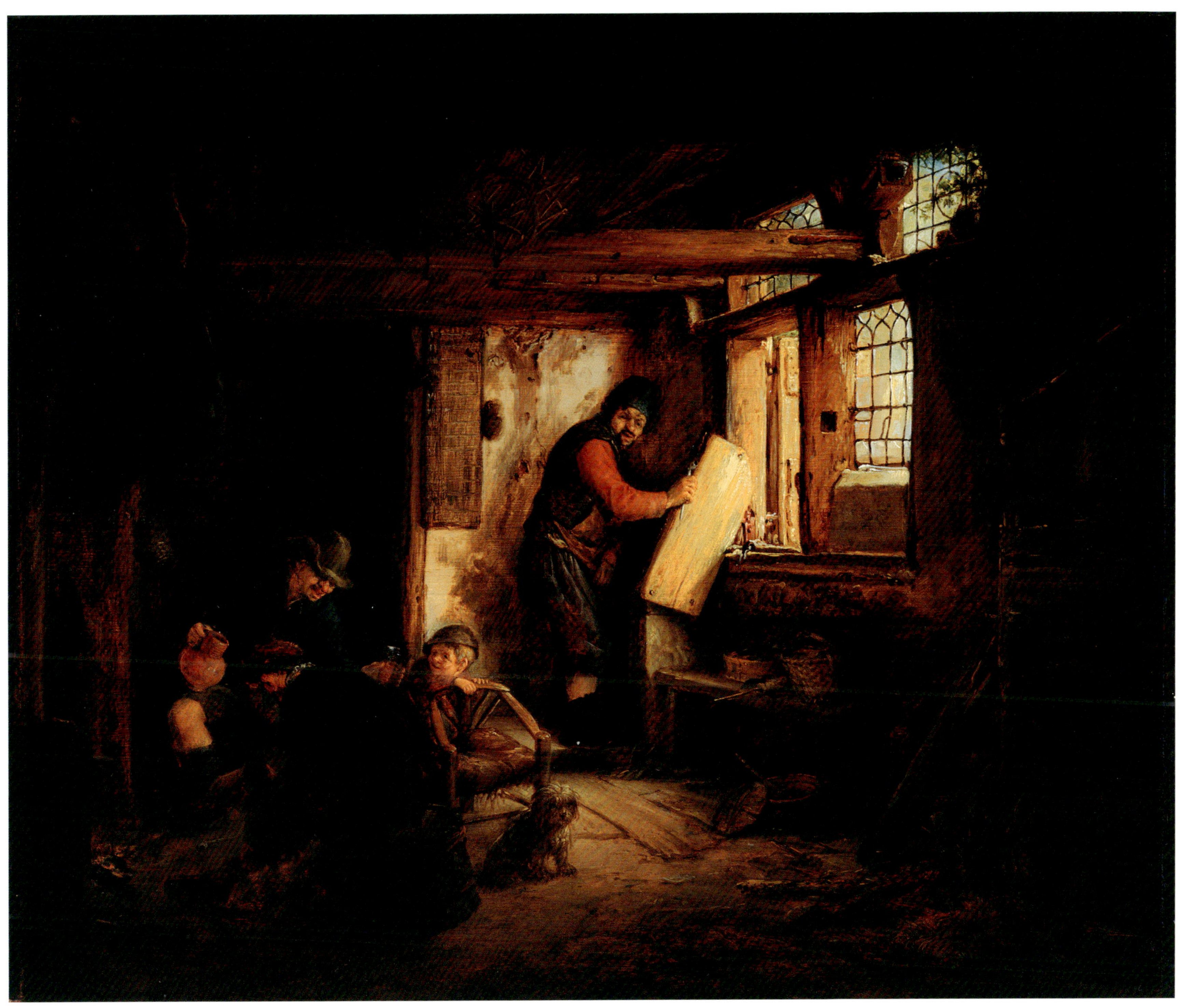

Adriaen van Ostade

7 *"Le Ménétrier" (The Violinist),* 1673

Oil on panel

45 x 42 cm

INSCRIBED: "A v Ostade. 1673"

Mauritshuis, The Hague

PROVENANCE: Govert van Slingelandt, The Hague, after 1752; Prince Willem V, The Hague, 1768–95; Mauritshuis, The Hague

BIBLIOGRAPHY: Rosenberg 1900, pp. 83–84, fig. 85; Hofstede de Groot 1907–28, vol. 3, p. 277, no. 429; Martin 1935–36, vol. 1, p. 394; Schnackenburg 1981, vol. 1, p. 125, no. 227; Hoetink 1985, pp. 240–41, illus, p. 413, no. 129; Broos 1994, pp. 74, 84, illus.

"Le Ménétrier" is a characteristic late work of the Haarlem peasant genre painter Adriaen van Ostade. Van Ostade's early works, influenced by his teacher Frans Hals and his fellow pupil the Flemish painter Adriaen Brouwer, typically portray peasants carousing or brawling in run-down taverns or barns; they are noted for their free brushwork and muted pale pinks and blues. By the 1660s, van Ostade's subjects and technique had changed considerably. His palette lightened and his attention shifted from raucous peasants to families harmoniously tending to daily life. As in this example, his scenes changed from dimly lit interiors to bright open-air settings. The later works often depict an outdoor gathering or a simple family laboring beneath the shade of a rough-hewn timber canopy.[1]

The present painting is one of van Ostade's most important works of the 1670s. The violinist, the boy beside him, who may be a hurdy-gurdy player, and the small children behind them form a group that is balanced on the right by a cluster of children, and just off center by a group peering out over the door.[2] The rhythmic gestures of the figures and their enthusiastic glances and facial expressions energize the composition and establish a carefully crafted system of counter-balances. Accents of strong color against an overall gray tonality also heighten the visual rhythms. The same lively cadences that one would hear from a violinist at a country fair are found in this accomplished late work.

Van Ostade painted *"Le Ménétrier"* near the end of a long and illustrious career that witnessed a gradual evolution from the riotous, seamy side of peasant life toward a more anecdotal and lyrical approach toward his subjects. The demeanor of these well-mannered farmers and tradesmen suggests conviviality and wholesome family values. This softer imagery has been attributed occasionally to the widowed artist's second marriage to an Amsterdam heiress in 1657.[3] Van Ostade, however, was well-to-do before this marriage and highly respected within the Haarlem artistic community. Rather, as Arthur Wheelock has pointed out, van Ostade's shifting attitude toward the peasant class may reflect larger sociological changes in Holland.[4] During the 1630s and 1640s, there were widespread assumptions that the lower echelon of society was "bestial or vulgar."[5] By the 1670s, the rural Dutch, who seemed unaffected by foreign influence and the taint of new wealth, came to represent "ideal virtues that were at the foundation of Dutch culture."[6] This nostalgic view of peasant virtues may have been heightened in van Ostade by his having to flee Haarlem for Amsterdam because of the French invasion of the Netherlands in 1672. *"Le Ménétrier"* was painted the year after, in 1673. LW

1 Hoetink 1985, p. 240.

2 Ibid..

3 Sullivan 1995, p. 148.

4 Wheelock 1995, pp. 189–99, and Hoetink 1985, p. 240.

5 Wheelock 1995, p. 189.

6 Ibid., p. 190. A watercolor of the same subject, also dated 1673, is in the Pierpont Morgan Library, inv. no. 134; Cornelis Ploos van Amstel made an engraving after it.

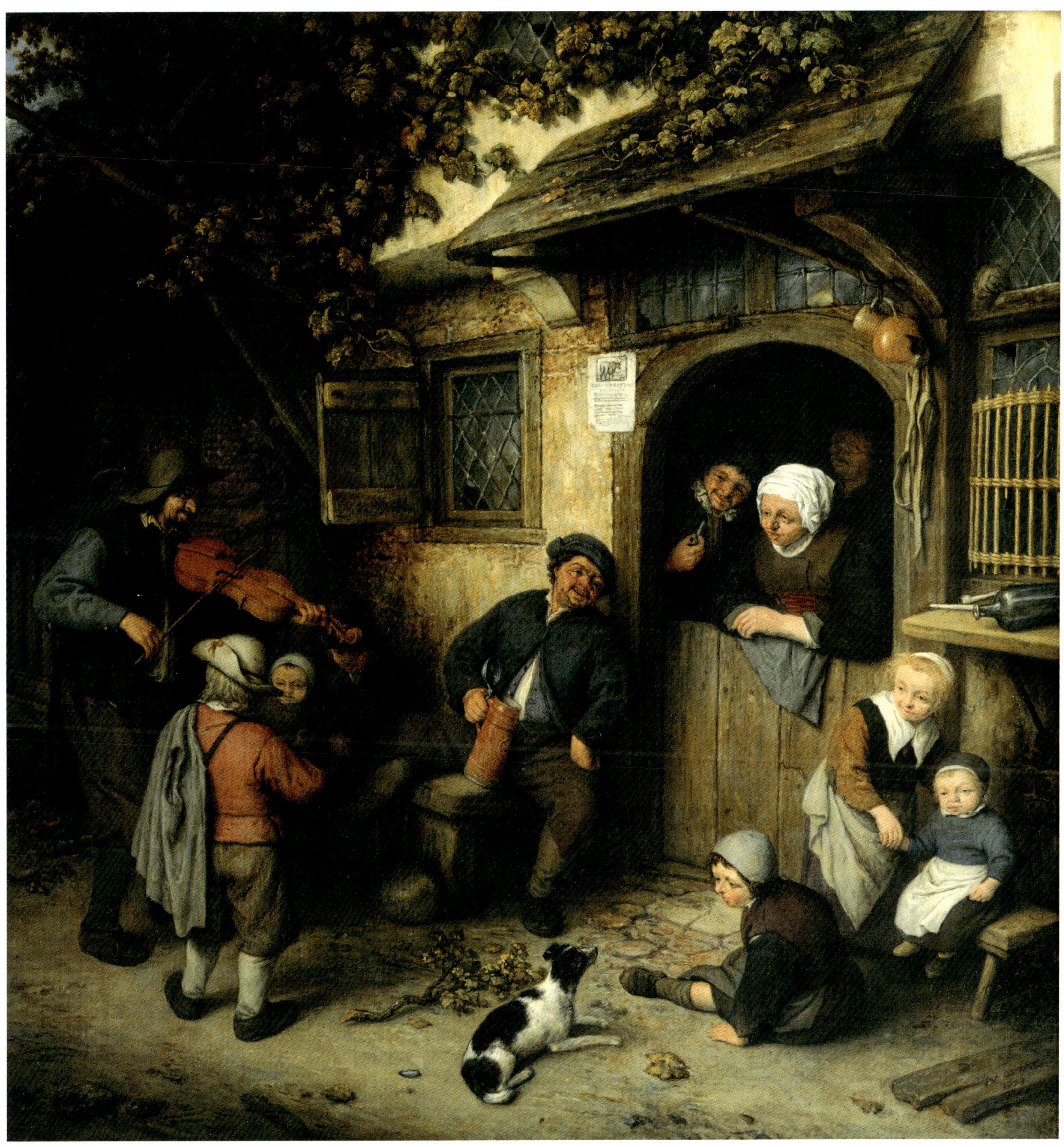

Philips Koninck

Amsterdam 1619–1688 Amsterdam

8 *Panoramic Landscape with Hunters,* c. 1665

Oil on canvas

105 x 135 cm

Private Collection

PROVENANCE: Lord Northwick, sale, Phillips, Cheltenham, Aug. 2, 1859, lot 433 (as S. de Koningh, *A Landscape with Distant Scenery*; to Weaver); Earl of Buckinghamshire, Hampden House, sale, Christie's, London, Mar. 17, 1890, lot 132 (as De Koning); Baron L. M. Herzog, Lesser, London; Budapest, 1911; seized by Hungarian authorities under German occupying forces in 1944; returned to Baronin Helene von Herzog in Basel probably around 1945; Rosenberg & Stiebel, New York; Private Collection, Schweinfurt; Galerie Kurt Meissner, Zurich, sale, Koller, Zurich, May 18–21, 1990, lot 5046; sale, Christie's, London, Dec. 11, 1992, lot 101; Private Collection

BIBLIOGRAPHY: London 1893, no. 23; Bierman 1912, pp. 421–23, fig. 7; Gerson 1936, p. 104, no. 16 (as Jacob Koninck); Raleigh 1956, p. 120, no. 56, illus.; Bernt 1970, vol. 2, no. 640, illus. (as Philips Koninck); Sumowski 1983–94, vol. 3, pp. 1534, 1548, no. 1063, p. 1613, illus. (as a variant on the painting cited by Gerson); vol. 6, p. 3619; New York 1995, pp. 85–89, no. 17, illus.

Around the age of eighteen, Philips Koninck registered as a pupil in the atelier of his brother Jacob in Rotterdam, where he remained for around three years.[1] He returned in the 1640s to his native Amsterdam to embark on a career as a painter of genre, history, and landscape.[2] He developed a loose and painterly handling incorporating direct brushstrokes, almost certainly from looking at paintings by Rembrandt, yet there is no evidence that he studied with the master. Nevertheless, as a brother-in-law to Abraham Furnerius and friend of Heymen Dullaert, both Rembrandt pupils, he did belong to his circle.[3] In 1658,

he assisted Rembrandt with his bankruptcy proceedings.[4] In turn, it was most likely Rembrandt who directed him to the work of the enigmatic Haarlem landscapist Hercules Seghers, who had exercised a profound influence on Rembrandt's conception of landscape, especially his tense, rhythmic patterns of highlights in touches of impasto.

Moving on from Rembrandt's monumental masses of landscape forms, Koninck developed a sophisticated vocabulary of devices to suggest space, including his distinctive, mesmerizing horizontal striations that mark successive planes receding into the distance. Koninck achieved great renown, such that Joost van den Vondel wrote verses on his paintings,[5] he was summoned to assist in the Uylenburgh affair in 1672,[6] and the Medicis acquired his *Self-Portrait* for their gallery.[7] While recognized in his own day for his history paintings and portraits, today he is considered one of the greatest landscape artists of the Dutch Golden Age—indeed, of any age.

In this present large canvas, Koninck applied his established formula of fields, rivers, and rows and clusters of trees and rural dwellings to a sweeping panoramic view. The foreground is dominated by the prominent motifs of a house in the left corner and a falconer and his servant on the road to the left of center. Receding diagonal lines, one of them formed by the banks of a river, imbue the recession into depth with energy. The dynamic quality carries through into the sky above, with its billowing cloud forms. The somber tones of the early years have given way to softer yellowish-browns, sharp greens, and pale blues, generating an ebullient overall effect.

When he published this painting in his monograph on Koninck, Horst Gerson assigned it to the artist's brother Jacob.[8] However, at that time, radical and unnecessary overpainting had affected its appearance, not only simplifying the composition and inserting trees to eliminate the foreground house, but repainting the clouds in more solid, abstract

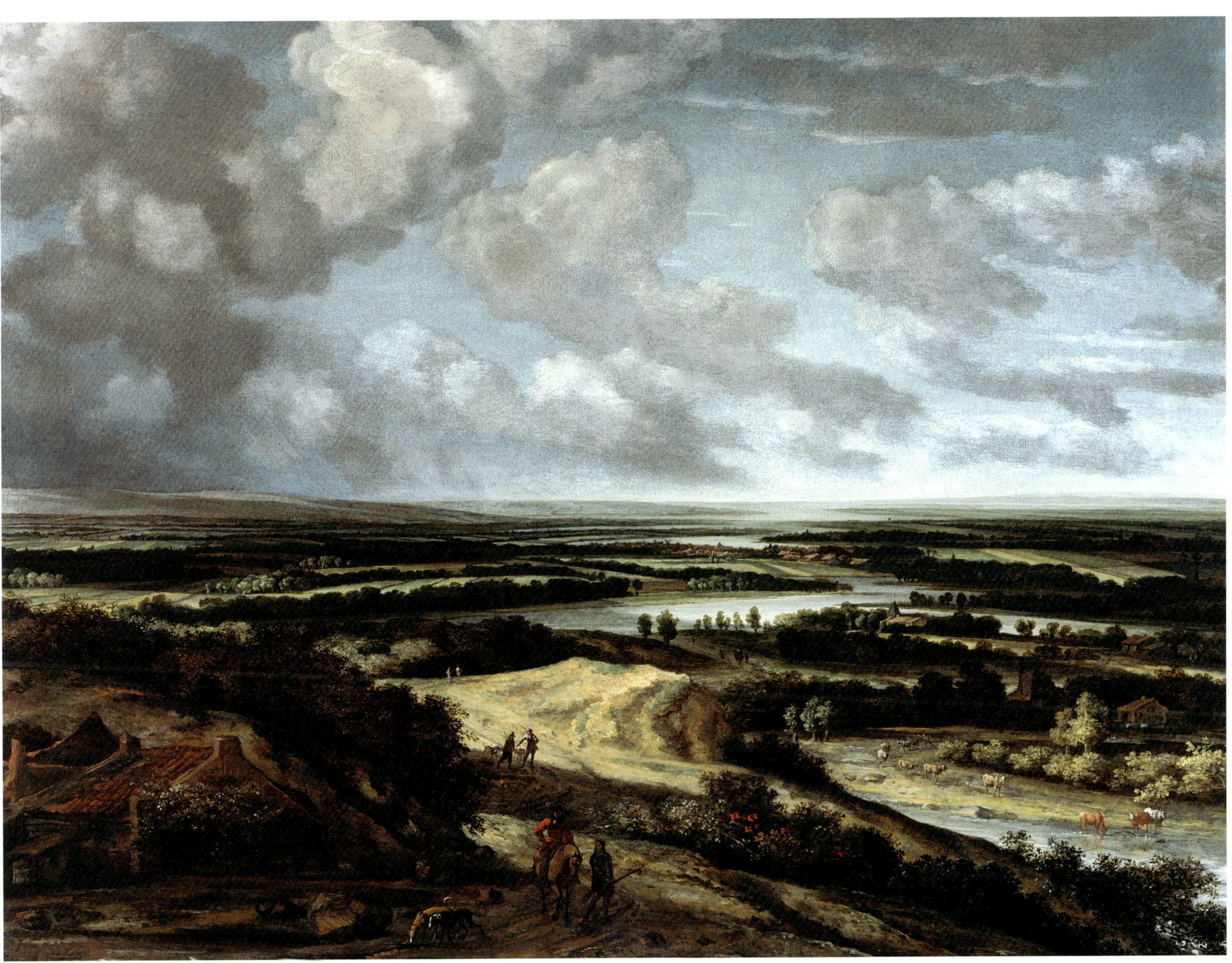

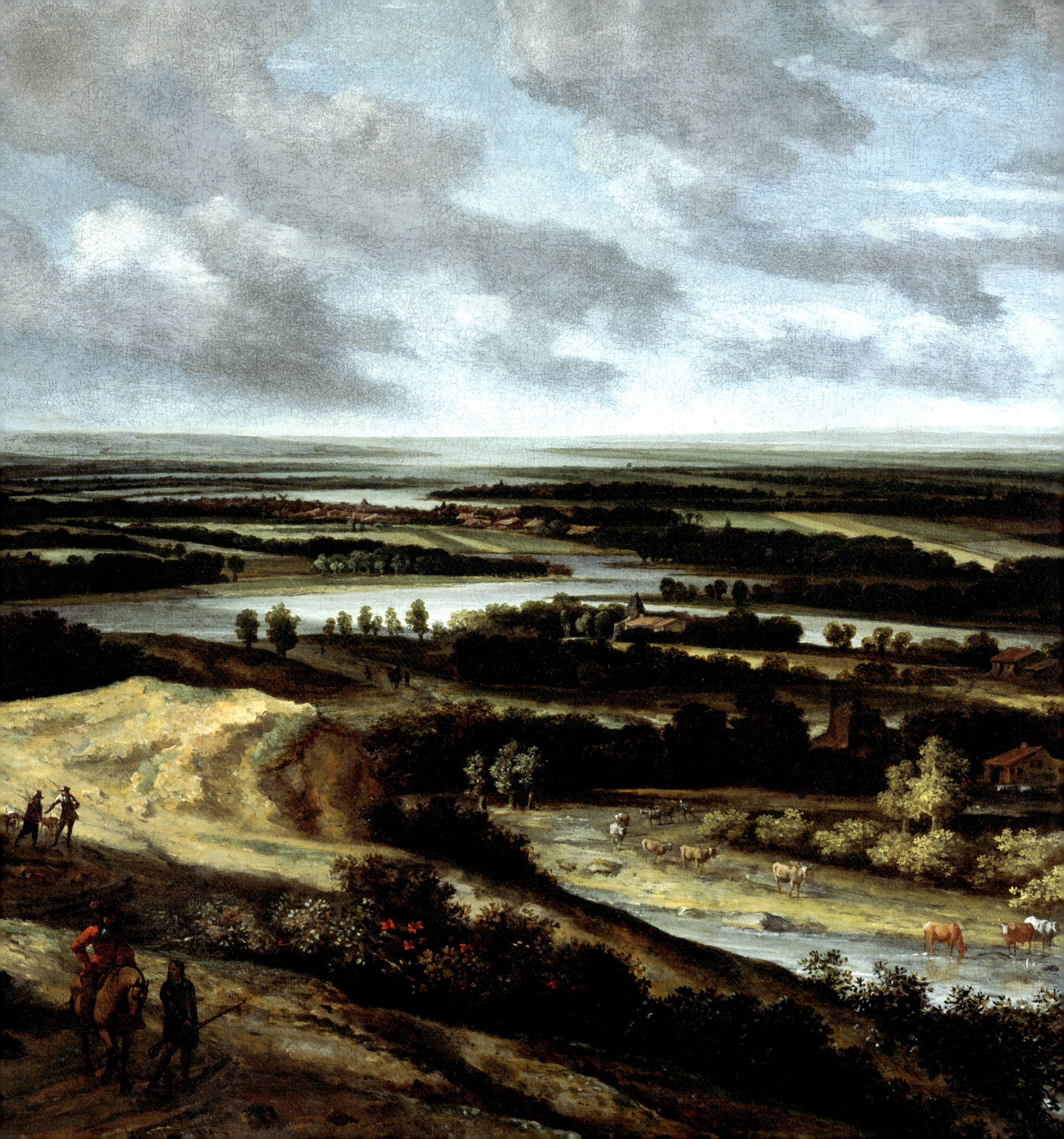

forms and thereby creating a modern and unrealistic appearance.
A general cleaning undertaken in 1954 by William Suhr uncovered the
foreground detail. It was not until a more recent cleaning by Charles
Munch that the area of the sky once again displayed the translucent
colors and free brushwork characteristic of Philips Koninck. A composition from 1664 in Rotterdam with similar features, such as the sandy
rise, the dale to the right, and the winding river, suggests a dating here
also to the mid-1660s.[9]

Peter Sutton pointed out a drawing in New York that appears
to have served as a study for the motif of the river winding through
the landscape in this painting.[10] The connection reveals Koninck's
working method of noting details of local landscape from life, then
using the sketches to conjure a fictional but convincing landscape in
his studio. Yet it is this artificial abundance of motifs, organized into
loose and dynamic rhythms, that gives this painting its captivating
and transcendent quality, and demonstrates why Philips Koninck
stands alongside Rembrandt and Jacob van Ruisdael as a master of
the Baroque landscape. DDW

1 Gerson 1936, p. 84, *Urkunde* no. 7d.

2 Gerson 1936, p. 58, *Urkunde* no. 11.

3 On his marriage to the sister of Furnerius, see: Gerson 1936, p. 84, *Urkunde* no. 10; on his
  friendship with Dullaert, see Sumowski 1983–94, vol. 1, p. 652. Koninck's portrait of Dullaert
  ranks among the finest of the Dutch Golden Age: oil on canvas, 63.5 x 55.9 cm, Saint Louis,
  Missouri, City Art Museum, inv. no. 408: 1923. See ibid., vol. 3, p. 1541, no. 1029, p. 1579,
  illus.

4 Gerson 1936, p. 10; Rembrandt Documents, pp. 440–42, no. 1659/11.

5 Gerson 1936, p. 92, *Urkunde* no. 58.

6 Ibid., p. 90, *Urkunde* no. 48.

7 *Self-Portrait with Antique Bust*, oil on canvas, 99 x 69 cm, signed and dated 1667, Florence,
  Galleria degli Uffizi, no. 448, acquired by Duke Cosimo III de' Medici during his visit to the
  Netherlands in the same year; see: Sumowski 1983–94, p. 1542, no. 1034, p. 1584, illus.

8 See Gerson 1936, p. 104.

9 *Landscape with a Sandy Rise*, oil on canvas, 95 x 121 cm, signed and dated 1664, Rotterdam,
  Museum Boijmans Van Beuningen, inv. no. 1419. The comparison was first put forward by
  Sumowski 1983–94, vol. 3, pp. 1548, no. 1060, p. 1610, illus.

10 Pen and brown ink, brown and gray washes, 19.4 x 31 cm, Paris, Fondation Custodia,
  inv. no. Frits Lugt Collection 1199. See Sumowski 1979–92, vol. 6, pp. 3030–31, no. 1357,
  illus.; Peter Sutton in New York 1995, p. 89.

Maerten de Cock

Antwerp 1578 (?)–1661 (?) Augsburg

9 *Coastal Mountain Landscape with Tobias and the Angel,* c. 1620s

Oil on copper

18.1 x 27 cm

INSCRIBED INDISTINCTLY AT LOWER RIGHT

Private Collection

PROVENANCE: Pasadena Art Museum; sale, Parke-Bernet, New York, Dec. 2, 1970, lot 27 (as attributed to Jan Velvet Brueghel); Private Collection

BIBLIOGRAPHY: Milwaukee 1976, pp. 142–43, no. 66, illus. (as Unknown Netherlandish Artist, around 1620)

Two young men walk along a high path set against an expansive sea below and a rocky coastline with mountains in the distance. The large fish carried by the younger man to the right identifies the scene as the Journey of Tobias from the apocryphal Book of Tobit (or Tobias). Tobias, sent by his father, Tobit, to collect a debt, receives help and guidance from the Archangel Raphael, disguised as a young man. When a large fish jumps from the water to attack him, Tobias is told to harvest its organs. These will expel a demon from his wife, Sarah, and cure his father's blindness.

Here, the artist followed a famous depiction by the German painter Adam Elsheimer, even to the unusual copper support.[1] Elsheimer in turn adapted the Flemish tradition of including fantasy figures as staffage in travel scenes. The reversed direction of the figures indicates that they were drawn not from Elsheimer's painting, but from a 1608 etching after it by Hendrick Goudt. A later print of 1613 is slightly different and likely follows a lost Elsheimer known in copies.[2] Goudt's etchings after Elsheimer were especially popular among artists in Amsterdam. De Cock slightly altered the figures and greatly reduced their scale to give prominence to the spectacular backdrop.

Despite the painting's traditional attribution to Jan Brueghel (1568–1625), the name of Maerten de Cock was first suggested in 1976 by Alfred Bader, and later confirmed by the remains of a signature.[3] This little-documented artist produced prints, paintings, and especially drawings; dated examples from 1620 to 1631 survive.[4] His three other known signed paintings are stylistically remarkably close to the present work.[5] The semitransparent glazes and penchant for fantasy alpine landscapes point to de Cock's origins in Antwerp, possibly studying in the Brueghel workshop. He likely followed artists such as David Vinckboons in seeking his fortune in the northern Netherlands. DDW

1 *Tobias and the Angel*, oil on copper, 12.4 x 19.2 cm, Frankfurt am Main, Frankfurt Historisches Museum, inv. no. B 789. See Andrews 1977, p. 150, no. 20, pl. 72.

2 *Tobias and the Angel ("The Small Tobias")*, 1608, etching, 13.4 x 18.5 cm. See Hollstein 1949–, vol. 8, p. 151, no. 1, illus. *Tobias and the Angel ("The Large Tobias")*, 1613, etching, 25.6 x 26.9 cm. See ibid., p. 152, no. 2, illus. For a painted copy, see *Tobias and the Angel*, oil on copper, 21 x 27 cm, Copenhagen, Statens Museum for Kunst, inv. no. Sp. 745. See Andrews 1977, p. 154, no. 25, pl. 89.

3 See Milwaukee 1976, pp. 142–43, no. 66, illus. The signature was discovered by Bert van Deun.

4 For an overview of the known works, see Le Bihan 1990, pp. 84–86, nos. 14–28, illus.

5 *Landscape with the Temple of the Sibyl at Tivoli*, 1620s, oil on wood, 27.5 x 42.6 cm, inscribed: "M. Cock Ft/162.," Bordeaux, Musée des Beaux-Arts de Bordeaux, inv. no. Bx E 464; Bx M 5697. See Le Bihan 1990, pp. 83–86, illus. *Mountainous River Landscape with a Fortress*, 1631, oil on wood, 28 x 44 cm, inscribed: "M. Cock Fecit 1631.24.01," Stockholm, Nationalmuseum, inv. no. NM 383. See Cavalli–Björkman 1990, p. 81, illus. *River Landscape with Gypsy Fortune Tellers*, oil on wood, 24.5 x 36 cm, signed: M. Cock Fe 16., formerly Paris, with J. O. Leegenhoek, in 1963. See Bernt 1970, vol. 1, no. 241, illus.

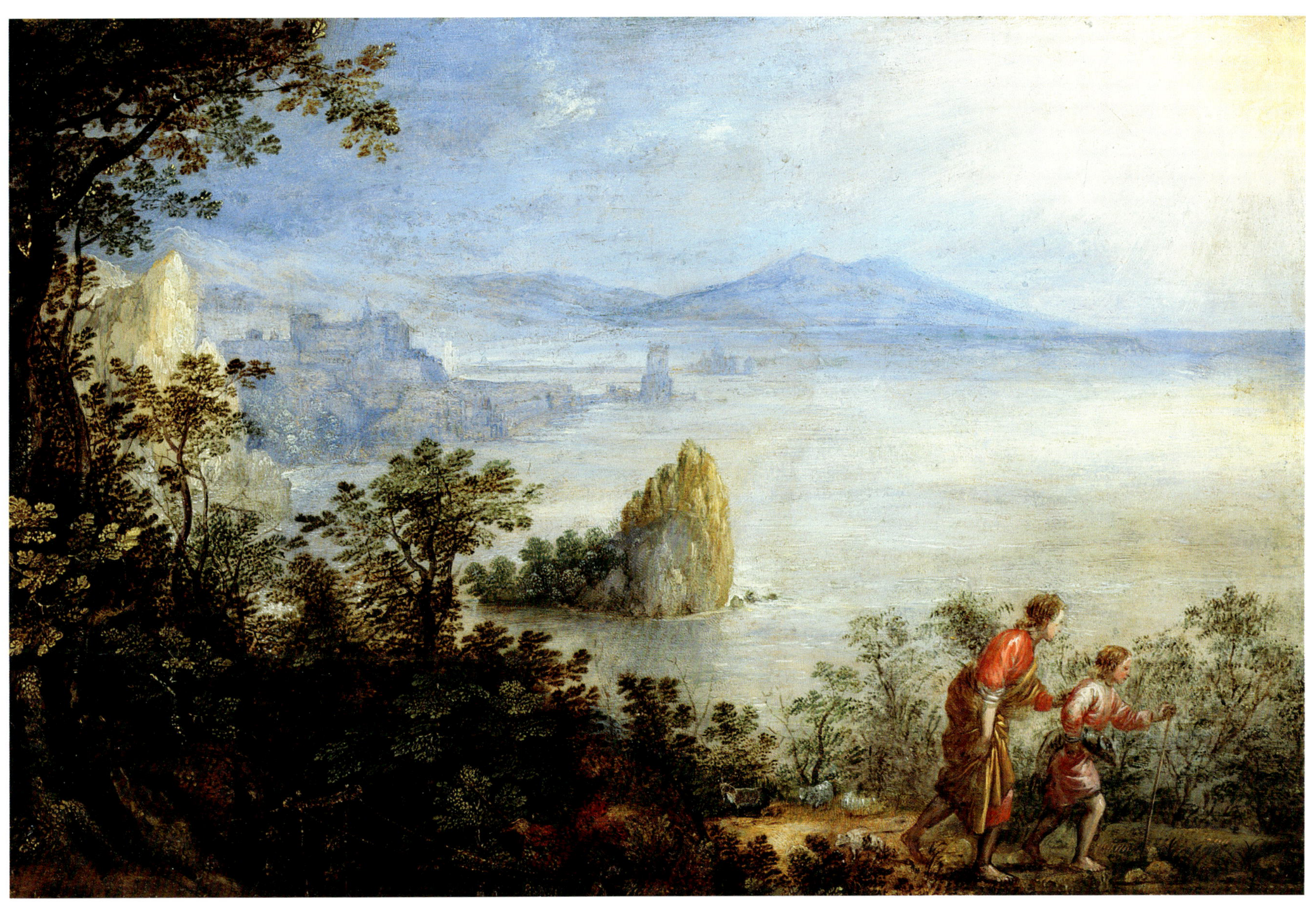

Gerbrand van den Eeckhout

Amsterdam 1621–1674 Amsterdam

10 *Rest on the Flight into Egypt,* 1653

Oil on canvas, 101 x 83.7 cm
INSCRIBED AT LOWER LEFT: "G. V. Eeckhout fc/ Ao 1653"
Private Collection
PROVENANCE: Captain Eric C. Palmer, Woburn Green; Private Collection
BIBLIOGRAPHY: London 1953, no. 24, illus.; Roy 1972, p. 216, no. 43
(as "Holy Family," fragment of a "Rest on the Flight into Egypt");
Sumowski 1983–94, vol. 2, p. 730, no. 415, p. 778, illus.

Arnold Houbraken, the near-contemporary chronicler of the Dutch
Golden Age, identified Gerbrand van den Eeckhout as a friend of
Rembrandt. Born in 1621 in Amsterdam to the goldsmith Jan Pietersz.
van den Eeckhout and his wife, Grietie Claes Lydeckers,[1] Eeckhout
likely trained in Rembrandt's studio in 1635–41.[2] Although he probably
studied alongside the pupils Govert Flinck and Ferdinand Bol, his
career took a path decidedly different from theirs. Instead of turning
toward the classicizing Flemish mode fashionable among Dutch nobility
and regents, Eeckhout continued to revisit a range of established
models in Rembrandt's own work and those favored by the master.
Old Testament themes predominate, although Eeckhout also depicted
genre subjects, including the "kortegard" or barracks scene. He main-
tained a strong light effect, and initially adhered to the monochromatic
range evident in Rembrandt's work and widely popular in the 1630s–40s,
though he soon began incorporating stronger hues, typically blue, in
the sky or in fabric. Such pictorial characteristics, as well as his stocky
figure type, derive from the work of Pieter Lastman and other earlier
Amsterdam artists known as the Pre-Rembrandtists, because they
helped shape the master's work.[3] This reference to Rembrandt constitutes
an homage and a declaration against prevailing fashion. Only in

Eeckhout's later works do classicizing aspects emerge, such as a larger
figure scale, elegant repose, and smooth abstraction of forms.

In this traditional representation of the Rest on the Flight into
Egypt, Mary carries the sleeping infant Jesus in her arms. With her left
hand, she uncovers his face, seemingly showing him to Joseph, who
peers in from behind. The empty landscape and the basket to the left
indicate that the Holy Family is pausing for a night's rest outdoors.
The threat of the Roman governor Herod's Massacre of the Innocents
adds an element of pathos to the familial scene.

The looming half-length figures filling the picture plane recall
a stylistic phase in Rembrandt's career in the mid-1630s that emphasized
figural monumentality. Likely familiar with such works from his time
in Rembrandt's studio, Eeckhout took Rembrandt's *The Holy Family*
(c. 1634) as the starting point for the present painting.[4] Eeckhout transformed his source, reversing the figure group and changing the view
of the heads of Mary and Joseph. Abandoning Rembrandt's domestic
interior, he set the scene outside at night and expanded the figures to
fill the frame. Quiet stillness replaces Rembrandt's bustling activity.
Mary's gesture of uncovering Jesus's head appears to come from another
work by Rembrandt, a print of the same theme dated 1645.[5] DDW

1 Thieme-Becker 1907–50, vol. 10, p. 354.

2 Sumowski 1983–94, vol. 2, p. 719.

3 Ibid.

4 Ibid., p. 730. Rembrandt, *The Holy Family*, c. 1634, oil on canvas, 183.5 x 123 cm, Munich,
   Alte Pinakothek; see Rembrandt Research Project 1983–, vol. 2, pp. 450–58, no. A88, illus.
   The same painting inspired a 1644 derivation by Eeckhout's fellow pupil Ferdinand Bol:
   The Holy Family, 1644, oil on canvas, 203 x 261 cm, Dresden, Gemäldegalerie, inv. no. 1603.
   See Sumowski 1983–94, vol. 1, p. 291, no. 81, p. 320, illus.

5 *Rest on the Flight into Egypt*, 1645, etching with touches of drypoint, 13 x 11.5 cm.
   See White and Boon 1969, vol. 1, p. 30, no. B58; vol. 2, p. 48, illus.

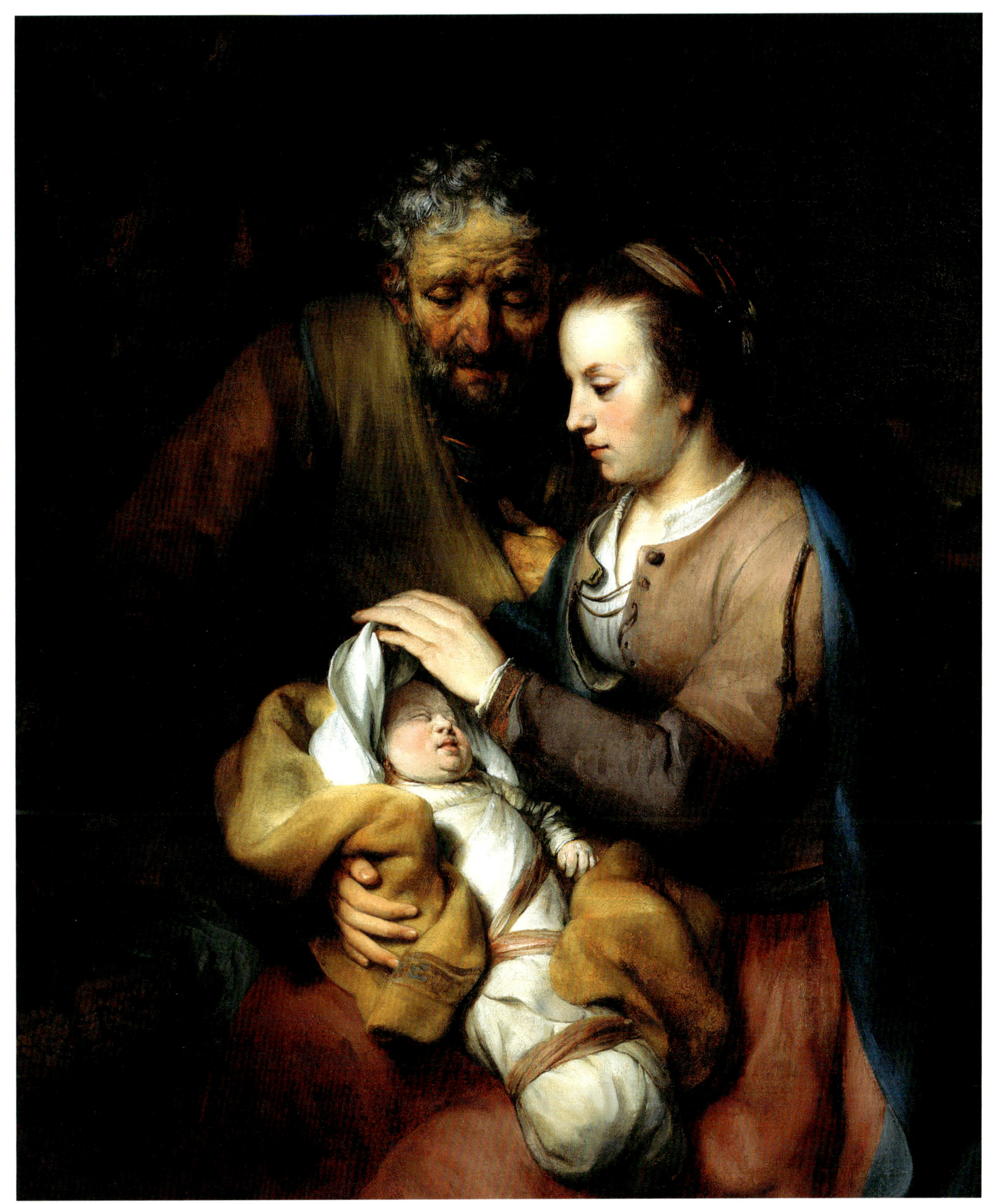

Allart van Everdingen

Alkmaar 1621–1675 Amsterdam

11 *Mountain Valley*, c. 1662

Oil on wood

25.5 x 39 cm

Traces of signature at lower right

Private Collection

PROVENANCE: Merlo sale, Heberle, Cologne, Dec. 9–11, 1891, lot 51 (as signed middle right); Erasmus, Berlin, 1931 (as fully signed); M. Bonn, Berlin; thence by descent, sale, Christie's, London, July 10, 1992, lot 127, illus.; Private Collection

BIBLIOGRAPHY: Raupp 1980, pp. 92, 107, n. 38; Davies 1978, p. 338 no. 84, pl. 193: Davies 2001, pp. 122, 237, no. 112, pl. 112

Allart van Everdingen was one of three sons from the second marriage of Pieter van Everdingen, a notary in Alkmaar, all of whom became painters. According to Houbraken, Allart, the youngest, first trained with the prominent Utrecht landscapist Roelant Savery.[1] Allart's earliest paintings, however, are seascapes, and likely reflect subsequent training with a specialist in this genre, perhaps Pieter Mulier in Haarlem.[2] Allart then studied with the Haarlem landscapist Pieter Molijn, probably between 1642 and 1644.[3] On a sea voyage to Scandinavia, a ship-wreck landed him in Norway. There he sketched the rugged forested landscape that was foreign to his eyes.[4] Returning in 1645 to his homeland, he became "The First Painter of Scandinavian Landscape," producing rocky forested scenes for the rest of his career. He joined his brother Cesar in Haarlem, entering the painters' guild and marrying in that city in 1645. The bustling market in Amsterdam drew him there in 1652. Competition from the prodigiously talented Jacob van Ruisdael and other painters who adapted his Scandinavian mode likely prompted van Everdingen to diversify in the 1660s, adding local landscape to his repertoire and developing himself as a printmaker.

Everdingen's scene of rocky promontories and castles is likely from the early 1660s; it demonstrates his increasing pursuit of structure and clarity and displays affinities with Mountain Village by Water, dated 1664.[5] Both show a thinner, more fluid handling of paint and a greater decorative richness than the dated landscapes of the mid-1650s.[6] The prominent compositional features—the rock pillars, cliff, and the castle—appear to have been adapted from his drawings, possibly made from life.[7] He may also have reworked the composition of a painting now in Budapest.[8] The present painting is distinguished, however, for the framing of a wide vista between two rises on either side, and a vast expanse of cloudy sky above. The resulting monumental effect strongly recalls the work of Hercules Seghers, which inspired many artists, including Rembrandt.[9] DDW

1 Houbraken 1717–21, vol. 2, pp. 95–96; for an English translation, see Davies 2001, p. 157. For the biography of Allart van Everdingen, see Davies 2001.

2 Huys Janssen 2001, p. 701.

3 Houbraken 1717–21, vol. 2, p. 95; Davies 2001, pp. 24–25.

4 See Houbraken 1717–21, vol. 2, p. 96; Davies 2001, pp. 26–27, 75, figs. 13–22.

5 Oil on wood, 31.7 x 48.1, signed and dated 1664, Montreal, Private Collection. See Davies 2001, pp. 122, 220–21, no. 44, pl. 44.

6 For example, *Norwegian Landscape*, 1656, oil on wood, 43.8 x 55.9 cm, Cambridge, Fitzwilliam Museum, inv. no. 66. See ibid., p. 220, no. 43, pl. 43.

7 Compare *Rocky Landscape*, pen and wash, brown and gray ink, 16.5 x 24.6 cm, London, British Museum, inv. no. 1836-8-11-178 and *Mountainous Landscape*, pen and ink, watercolor, 11.5 x 16.8 cm, Cambridge, Fitzwilliam Museum, inv. no. PD 323-1963. See ibid., figs. 104, 140.

8 Oil on canvas, 85.7 x 113 cm, Budapest, Museum of Fine Arts, inv. no. 210. See ibid., p. 237, no. 111, pl. 111.

9 Hercules Seghers, *Rocky Mountain Landscape*, oil on canvas, mounted onto wood, 55 x 100 cm, Florence, Galleria degli Uffizi, inv. no. 77.254. See Chiarini 1989, pp. 524–26, illus.

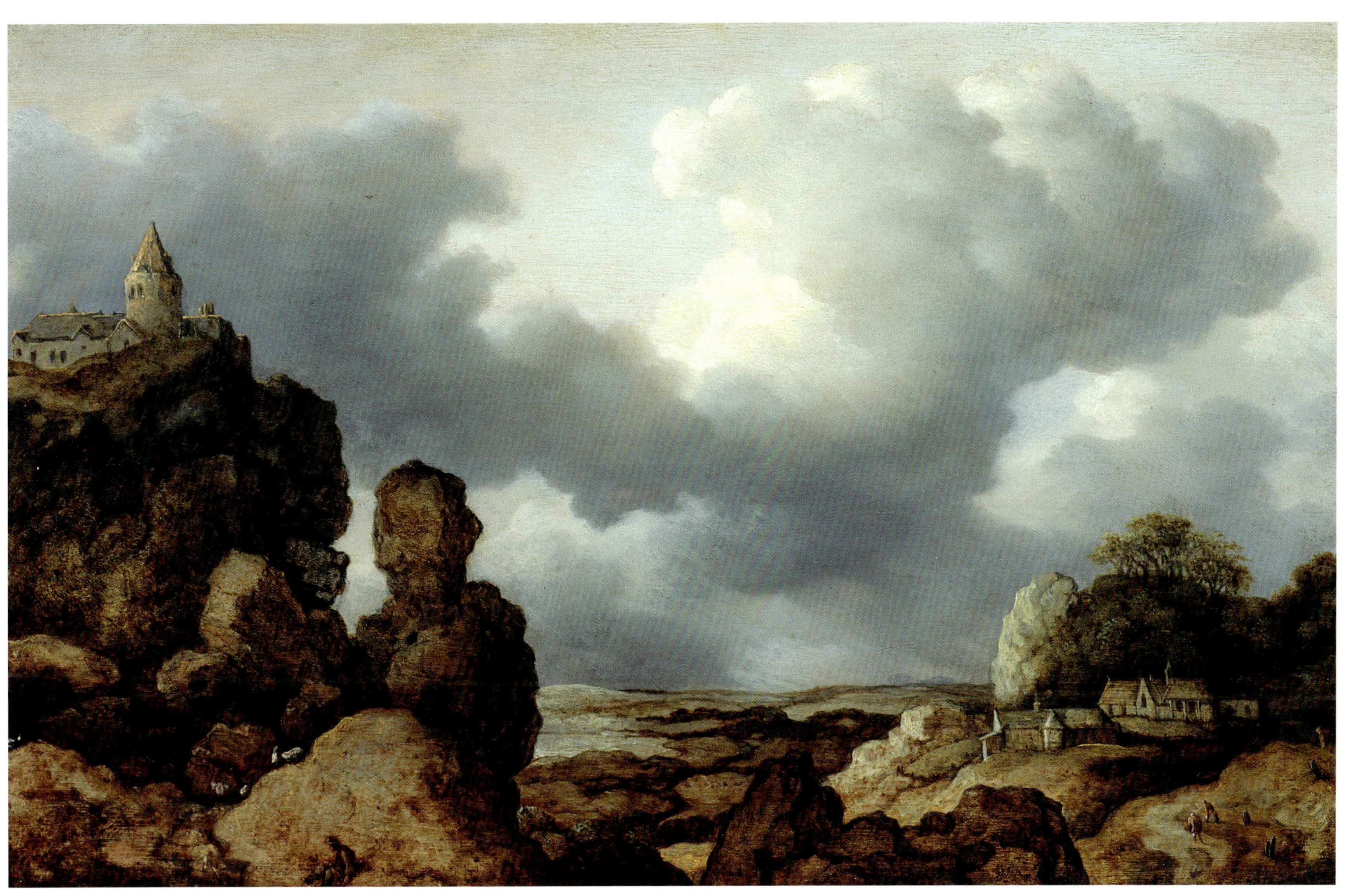

Karel Dujardin

Amsterdam 1628–1678 Venice

12 *Landscape with an Italian Town,* c. 1675–78

Oil on canvas

45 x 58.5 cm

Private Collection

PROVENANCE: sale, Sotheby's London, June 11, 1969, lot 87 (as Jan Asselyn); sale, Phillips, London, July 2, 1996, lot 7, illus. (as Circle of Adriaen van der Cabel); Clovis Whitfield Fine Art, London; Private Collection

BIBLIOGRAPHY: none known

Karel Dujardin enjoys a reputation as one of the most accomplished Dutch painters of Italianate landscape. Although his training is not known, his early paintings closely follow the style of the Haarlem Italianizing specialist Nicolaes Berchem, with whom he likely studied. Houbraken relates a colorful story of the young Dujardin's consent to a marriage proposal from a woman innkeeper to whom he owed money.[1] The biographer also tells of his membership in the "Bentveughels" in Rome, where he was given the nickname "Bokkebaart" ("Goat's Beard").[2] A signed and dated drawing of a piazza in Rome appears to indicate that his Roman stay took place in the years 1652–55 and not in the 1640s, as Houbraken asserts.[3] In 1656, he became a founding member of the newly established painters' confraternity "De Pictura" in The Hague; three years later, he was in Amsterdam.[4] Known for applying a smooth finish enlivened with a strong light, Dujardin also achieved success as a portrait and history painter in addition to his landscapes. In 1675, he accompanied the collector and patron Jan Reynst to Italy, first visiting Rome and then proceeding to Venice, where the artist died in 1678.[5]

His second sojourn in Italy inspired Dujardin to renewed vibrancy in his depiction of the Italian landscape. This scene of a walled town with a high tower exemplifies his style of this period in its powerful rendering of tone and surface in smoothly applied impasto layers, which replaced the thinner technique of his Amsterdam years. The late compositions conjure monumental landscapes peopled with travelers; mountain forms loom in the distance and figures of reduced scale are placed within, rather than in front of, their surroundings.[6] One such painting, now in Vienna, also incorporates a distant view of a town on a hill.[7] The present picture is an exception among Dujardin's late Italian paintings in presenting a view of a town at such close range. At the same time, its magisterial presence, dwarfing the figures before it, and echoed in the mountains behind, is entirely in keeping with the transcendent calm that characterizes this phase of the artist's career. DDW

1 Houbraken 1717–21, vol. 3, p. 60.

2 Ibid., p. 56.

3 Two documents place Dujardin in Amsterdam in 1652 and 1655. See Edouard Plietzsche in Thieme-Becker 1907–50, vol. 10, p. 103. An inscription on one of his drawings identifies its Roman site. See Schatborn 2001, p. 154.

4 Saur 1999–, vol. 30, p. 422.

5 Houbraken 1717–21, vol. 3, pp. 59–60.

6 Oil on canvas, 54.2 x 72.4 cm, sale, Sotheby's Amsterdam, May 3, 1999, lot 48, illus. Oil on wood, 90.3 x 115.5 cm, private collection. See London 2002, pp. 150–51, no. 35, illus.

7 Oil on canvas, 53 x 68.5 cm, Vienna, Gemäldegalerie der Akademie der bildenden Künste, inv. no. 827. See ibid., pp. 152–53, no. 36, illus.

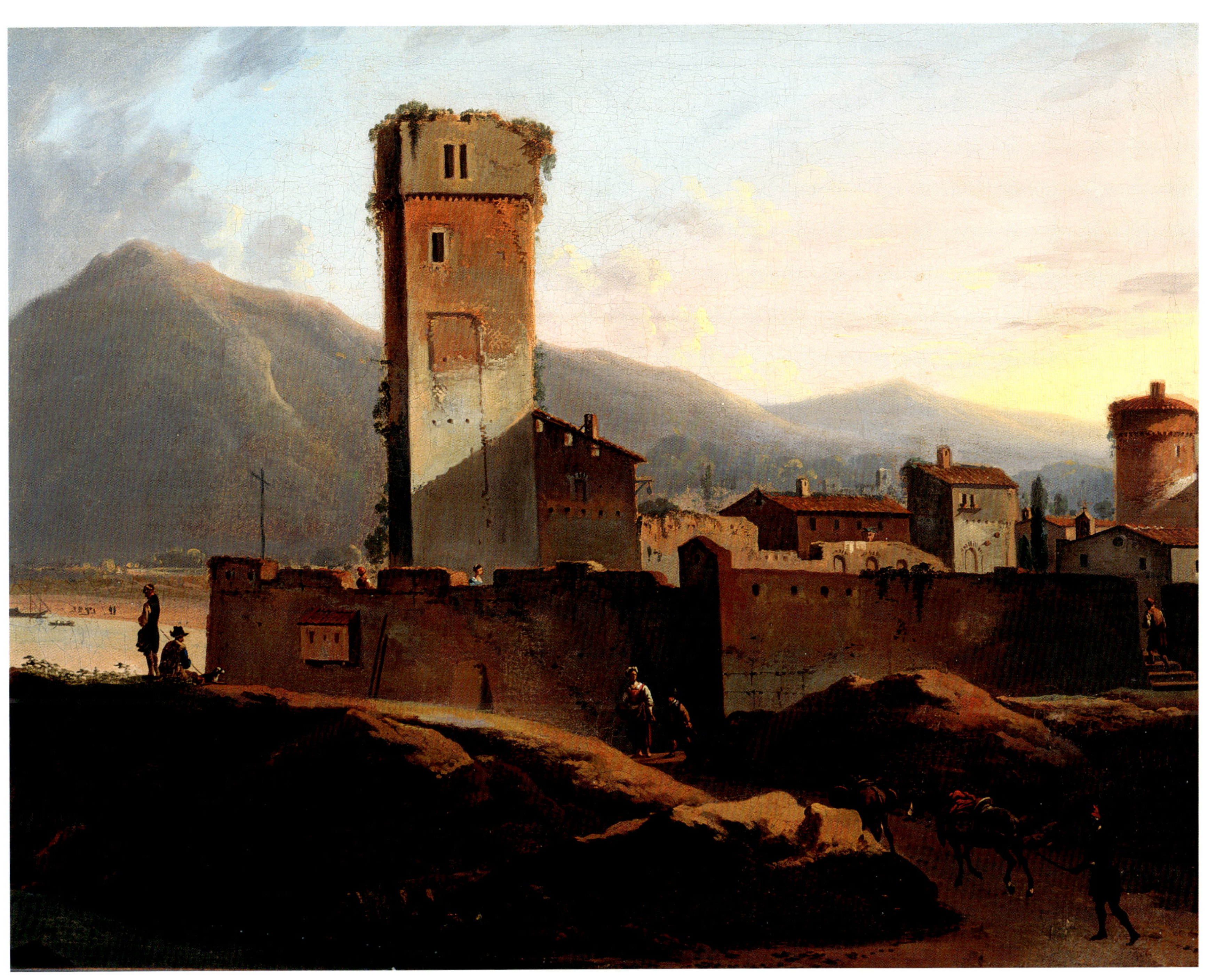

Jacob van Ruisdael

HAARLEM 1628/29–1682 AMSTERDAM

13 *Winter Landscape,* c. late 1660s

Oil on canvas
35.5 x 31.1 cm (mounted on supporting canvas measuring
38.6 x 33.3 cm)
Private Collection
INSCRIBED AT LOWER LEFT: "J. V. Ruysdael"
PROVENANCE: Max Steinthal, Berlin, c. 1890–1906; Major J. C. F. Gundry,
The Hyde, Walditch, Bridport, Dorset; sale, Christie's, London, Dec. 11,
1984, lot 21, illus. (as indistinctly signed); Private Collection
BIBLIOGRAPHY: Berlin 1890, p. 55, no. 253; Bode 1890, pp. 237–38;
Berlin 1906, p. 32, no. 120; Hofstede de Groot 1908–27, vol. 4, p. 308,
no. 988; Rosenberg 1928, p. 110, no. 606; Bader 1985, p. 85, illus.;
Slive 2001, p. 479, no. 682, illus.

Already in his earliest landscapes, produced around the age of seven-
teen, Jacob van Ruisdael transformed the restrained Haarlem tradition,
imbuing it with the drama of the high Baroque and achieving
a parallel to the history paintings of Rembrandt.[1] Ruisdael was reared
in an artistic family living in a cultural center. His father, Isaack, was
a painter, framer, and art dealer,[2] and his uncle and cousin were
landscape painters. Jacob almost certainly received instruction from
his famous uncle Salomon in the early 1640s in Haarlem, where he
joined the guild in 1648.[3] A keen interest in woods and forests
distinguishes his earliest works from those of his uncle, and likely
reflects a cultivated knowledge of the earlier Flemish tradition for
forest scenes. In the 1650s, Ruisdael traveled extensively in Holland,
and is known to have visited the German region of Westphalia with
his friend and fellow landscape painter Nicolaes Berchem.[4] By 1657,
likely in pursuit of a better market for his paintings,[5] he had moved
to Amsterdam, where he remained for the rest of his life.

The numerous winter landscapes Ruisdael painted over the
course of his career all tend to emphasize the dark and threatening
aspect of the season—a stark contrast to the levity that Pieter Bruegel
and his followers evoked in the same specialty.[6] In the present example,
a large rural dwelling toward the right dominates the composition.
In the foreground in front of it, a couple accompanied by a dog walk
toward the viewer. Balancing these motifs are a bare tree arching in
from the left edge with a thatched shed behind it. The space between
the two buildings reveals a distant field. The dark cast of a cloud-
covered early evening dominates the scene. Accented with patches of
snow, the house and the tree assume a monumental, bleak presence
against the somber background. The two figures, bent over and
confined to the bottom of the composition, seem to express the
oppression and desolation of their surroundings. The billowing and
twisting dark clouds above promise only more inhospitable weather.

Among the nearly seven hundred works he gives to Ruisdael,
Seymour Slive includes thirty-two winter landscapes. In its monumen-
tality and painterly handling, the present example is closest to *Winter
Landscape with a Broken Bridge*, formerly in Holsteinborg, and *Winter
Landscape* in the Mauritshuis, works that Slive dates to the 1660s.[7]
The same date can tentatively be assigned to the present work. DDW

1 For an overview of Ruisdael's achievement, see "Ruisdael's Critics," in Walford 1991,
   pp. 186–202.

2 On Isaack van Ruisdael's career, see Giltaij 1992.

3 Miedema 1980, vol. 2, pp. 933, 1037.

4 Büttner and Unverfehrt 1993.

5 Wijnmann 1932, p. 179.

6 Stechow 1966, p. 97; Bader 1985, p. 85, illus.

7 *Winter Landscape with a Broken Bridge*, oil on canvas, 35 x 31 cm, Amsterdam art market,
   1993. See Slive 2001, p. 475, no. 675, illus. (as 1660s). *Winter Landscape*, oil on canvas,
   37.3 x 32.5 cm, The Hague, Mauritshuis, inv. no. 802. See ibid., p. 474, no. 673, illus. (as 1660s).

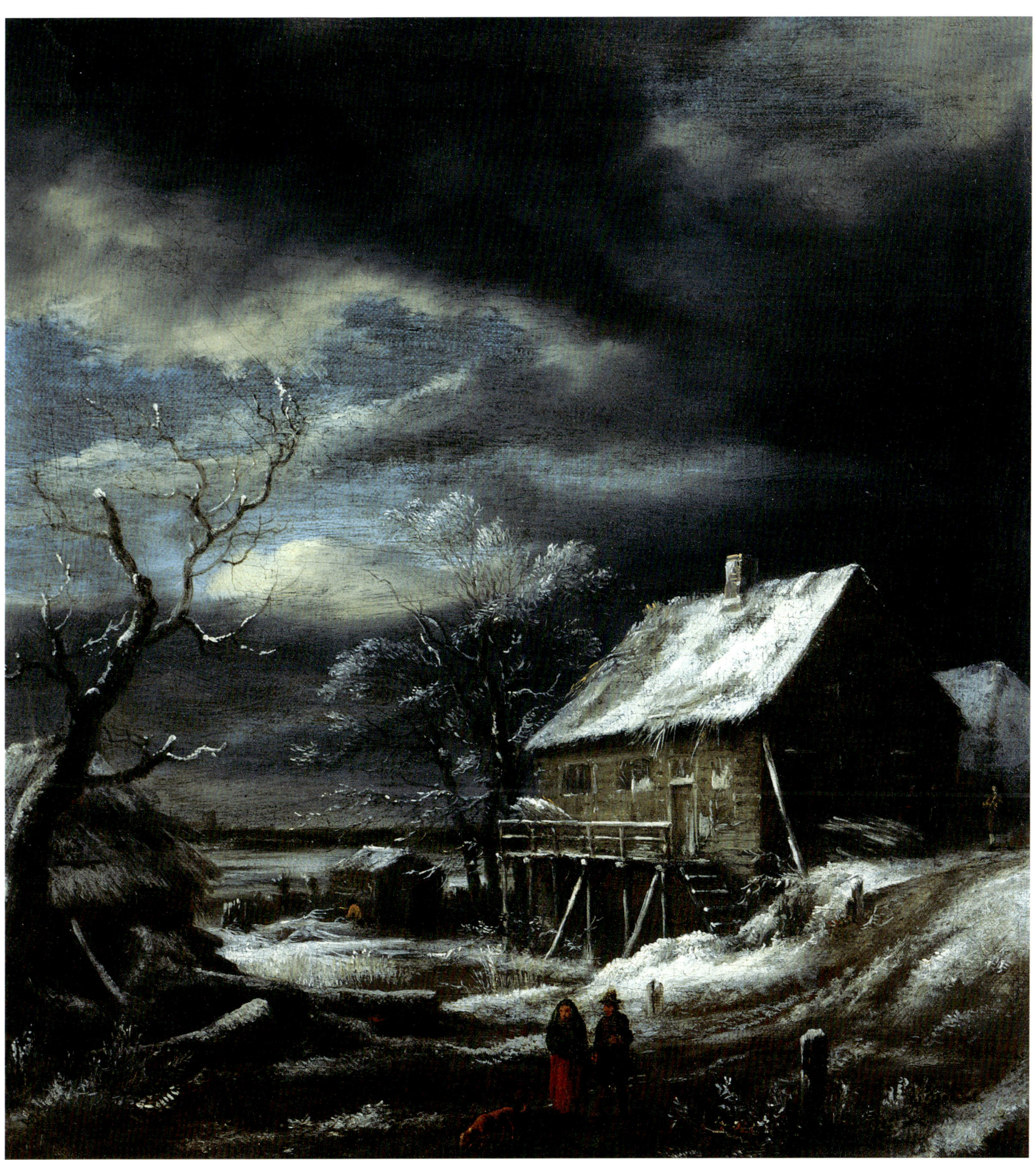

Ludolf Bakhuizen (Backhuysen)

EMDEN 1631–1708 AMSTERDAM

14 *Fishing Vessels Offshore in a Heavy Sea,* 1684

Oil on canvas

64.6 x 97.7 cm

INSCRIBED ON THE BARREL AT LEFT: "L. Backh. 1684"

The Minneapolis Institute of Arts, Gift of John Hawley, by exchange, inv. no. 82.84

PROVENANCE: Collection Mrs. Barnard, sale, Christie's, London, June 12, 1925, lot 32; Collings, by 1925; sale, Galerie Commeter, Hamburg, April 27, 1940, lot 3, illus.; sale, Christie's, London, July 10, 1981, lot 17, illus.; Richard Green and Douwes Fine Art, London; The Minneapolis Institute of Arts

BIBLIOGRAPHY: Houbraken, vol. 2, pp. 236-244; Smith 1835, vol. 6, pp. 401–458; Hofstede de Groot 1907–27, vol. 7, pp. 211–322; Preston 1937, pp. 48-49; Minneapolis 1988, p. 102, illus.; Amsterdam 1985; Nannen 1985; Paris 1989, 133-134; Minneapolis/Toledo/Los Angeles 1990–91, pp. 82–97, 402–403, no. 2, illus.

The sea was one of the key factors in the booming Dutch culture of the seventeenth century. It provided the Dutch with a great variety of food and was a vital element in their flourishing economic development. It was the stage for their naval battles and the economic highway that allowed them to become a center of world trade. The sea was at times both their greatest friend and their greatest foe—a constant threat to their land and sometimes their very lives.

Ludolf Bakhuizen painted *Fishing Vessels Offshore in a Heavy Sea* in 1684 at the high point of his career. He focused on two single-masted sailboats on a windy day, with storm clouds looming in the sky. The fishing boats heel in the gusts, as the one on the left comes to the aid of the other, which has torn its mainsail. Sailors struggle to gain control of the damaged vessel as a huge wave surging beneath their prows suddenly endangers them both. Barrels bob ominously in the water, suggesting that the outcome of the rescue is far from certain. Several other vessels are visible in the distance; a third fishing boat races on a rising swell to assist the beleaguered vessels, while a large merchant ship heads to sea to ride out the storm.[1]

Bakhuizen is noted for his dramatic scenes with churning waters, billowing storm clouds, stark contrasts of light and dark, and tossing ships in peril. The majority of his paintings depict ships just offshore, either outside the port of Amsterdam or near the island of Texel, north of the Zuider Zee. One favorite compositional formula was to place sailboats in open water with land appearing only in the distance. The present work's distant sand dunes at the left may be those of Den Helder across from the island of Texel and close to the mouth of the Zuider Zee, a location he returned to many times during his career.[2]

Bakhuizen was familiar with such scenes from having worked in his youth as a shipping clerk in the small German port of Emden. At the age of eighteen, he moved with his family to Amsterdam, where he studied with marine painters Allart van Everdingen (1621–1675) and Hendrick Dubbels (1620/21–1693). In 1656, he was listed as a member of Kalligraphie, a penmanship society, and his earliest works are actually "penwerken" ("pen-paintings") and grisaille paintings on panel.[3] Although Willem van de Velde the Elder had used this medium with great success, Bakhuizen soon turned to conventional painting. After van de Velde and his son Willem van de Velde the Younger immigrated to England in 1672/73, he became the leading seascape painter in the Netherlands. LW

1 Minneapolis/Toledo/Los Angeles 1990–91, pp. 82–84, no. 2.

2 Ibid., p. 82. For biographical background, see Hofstede de Groot 1907–27, vol. 7, pp. 211–322.

3 Wheelock 1995, pp. 14–15.

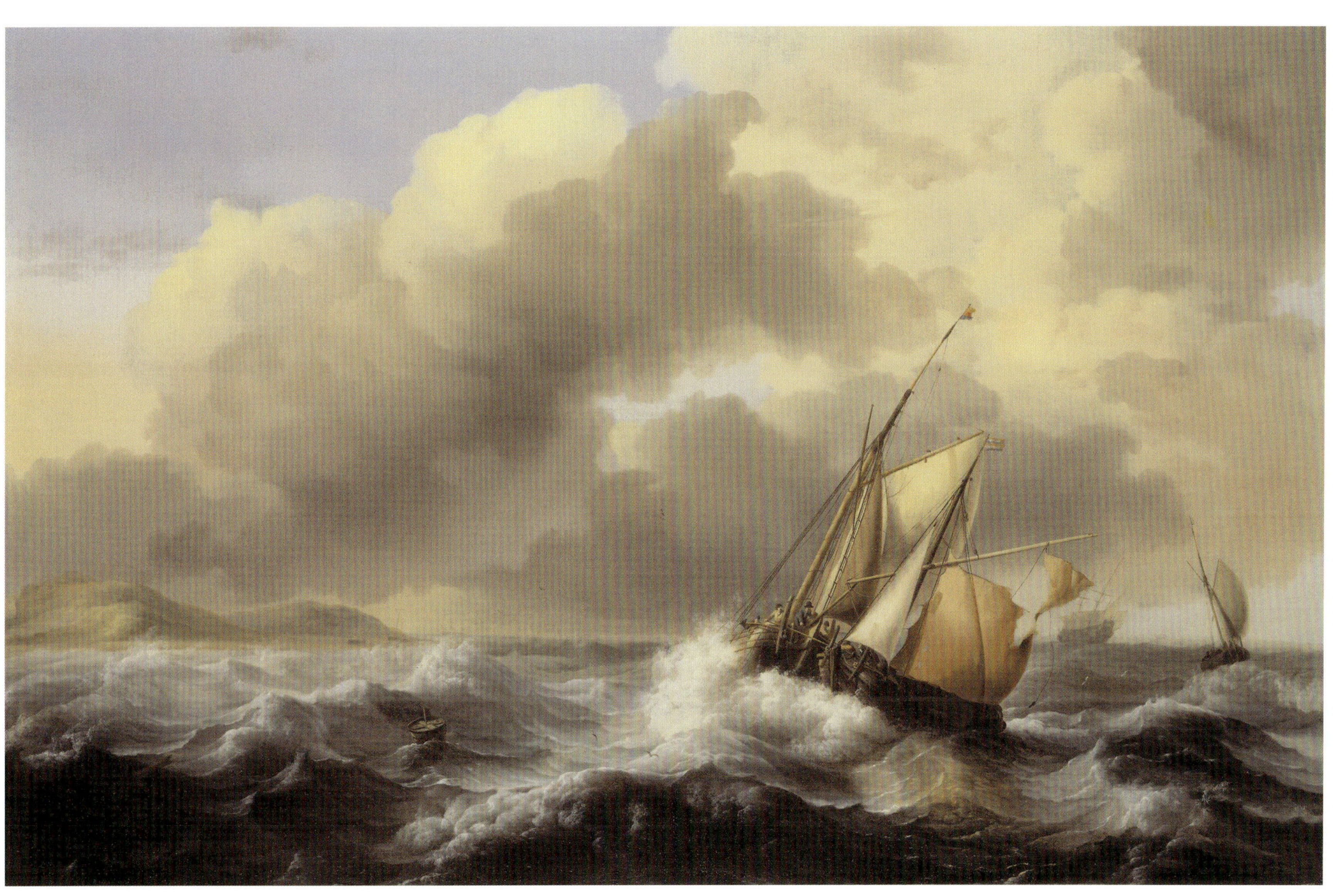

Willem van de Velde the Younger

Leiden 1633–1707 London

15 *A Dutch Ship at Anchor Drying Sails and a Kaag under Sail*, c. 1660

Oil on canvas

68.7 x 92 cm

Inscribed: Traces of a signature between the stock of the port anchor and the warp leading to it

Collection of Mr. and Mrs. Frederick Vogel III, Milwaukee

Provenance: Sir Henry Houghton; P.A.B. Widener, Philadelphia; Bachstitz Gallery, The Hague; Ralph H. Booth, 1925; bequest to Virginia Booth Vogel, 1931; Mr. and Mrs. Frederick Vogel III, Milwaukee

Bibliography: Smith 1835, vol. 6, pp. 313–400; Haverkorn van Rijsewijk 1901, vol. 19, pp. 61–63; Hofstede de Groot 1907–27, vol. 7, pp. 1–73; Willis 1911, pp. 79–89; Hofstede de Groot and Valentiner 1913, illus.; Bachstitz n.d., vol. 3, pl. 98; Bachstitz 1923; Burlington 1924, p. iv, and 1925, p. vi; Robinson 1958–74; MacLaren 1960, pp. 429–21; Bol 1973, pp. 241–43; Preston 1974, pp. 52–57; Greenwich 1982; Paris 1989, p. 149; Robinson 1990, vol. 1, pp. 265–68, no. 13, illus.; LaWall Lipshultz 1990, pp. 160–76, 420–22

Willem van de Velde the Younger came from a gifted family of artists. His brother Adriaen van de Velde (1636–1672) was a noted landscape painter, and his father, Willem van de Velde the Elder, was famous for his detailed drawings and pen paintings of ships. Willem the Younger first studied with his father and then with Simon de Vlieger (1600/1601–1653), one of the chief exponents of tonal painting at mid-century.[1] Willem the Younger went on to achieve in his paintings an ideal balance between a meticulous depiction of ships and a delicate, poetic rendering of light and atmosphere. His masterful control of space made him the greatest Dutch marine painter of the seventeenth century.

In the early 1660s, Willem the Younger had begun to paint vessels on calm waters with light breezes. In all of these paintings, known as "calms"—whether of sailboats by jetties or ships on a glassy sea—the artist transformed the silvery atmospheric effects of Simon de Vlieger into a soft, unifying transparent light that attains a new level of subtlety. In later years, he followed the general tendency in Dutch art toward more colorful, brighter pictures, maintaining a consistently high standard throughout his more than six hundred paintings.[2]

In *A Dutch Ship at Anchor Drying Sails and a Kaag under Sail*, which probably dates from the early 1660s, the interplay of color and light creates an impressive spatial effect.[3] Although the ships are depicted with painstaking accuracy, the artist has not allowed himself to become lost in detail. The combination of soft tonal contrast with a few highlights of local color gives the painting a rare harmony. On the left is a kaag with a small boat grappled to its starboard; a light breeze just fills the kaag's topsail. To the right is a majestic ship at rest, her topsails gently sagging. The ship flies the flag of a Dutch merchant ship. Various vessels in the background include a Dutch flute seen partially behind the starboard, and on the far left, an English hooker.

In the winter of 1672/73, a year of political and military turmoil for the Dutch Republic, the Elder and Younger van de Veldes left for England, where they reconstituted their atelier and entered the service of King Charles II and the Duke of York.[4] After their move to London, Willem the Younger's works shifted from nonhistorical maritime subjects to commissioned representations of recent English naval victories, in keeping with the interests of his royal patrons. LW

1 For biographical information, see Robinson 1990, vol. 1, pp. ix-xxvi, and LaWall Lipshultz 1990, pp. 420–22.

2 Minneapolis/Toledo/Los Angeles 1990–91, p. 421.

3 See Robinson 1990, vol. 1, pp. 265–269, for a full description of the painting's subject.

4 LaWall Lipshultz 1990, p. 421.

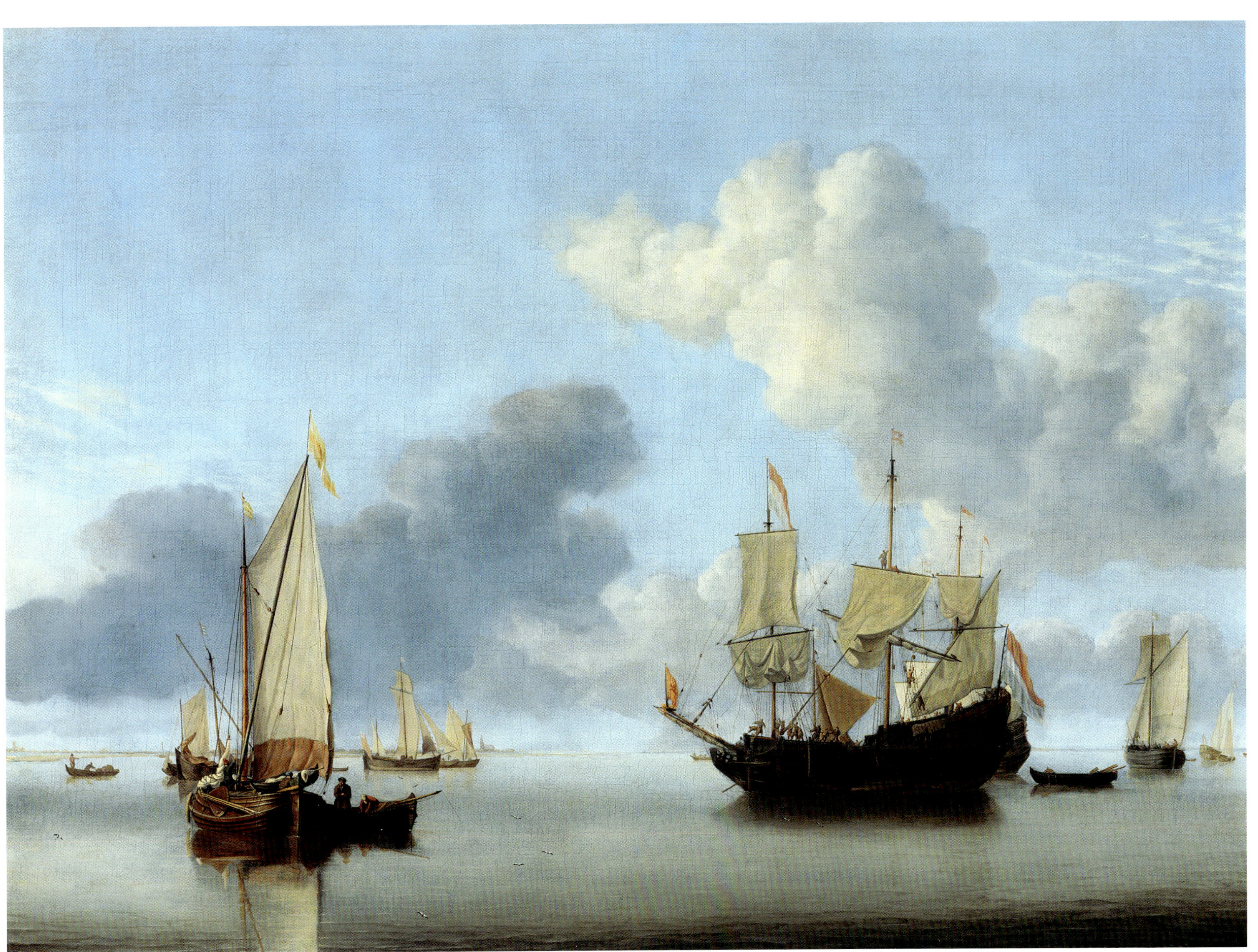

SELECTED BIBLIOGRAPHY

AUTHORS

Andrews 1977
Andrews, K. *Adam Elsheimer*. New York, 1977.

ARTnews 1954
ARTnews 1954, p. 42, illus.

Bachstitz n.d.
Bachstitz Gallery, vol. 3, pl. 98.

Bachstitz 1923
Bachstitz Gallery *Bulletin*, October.

Bader 1985
Bader, A. "About Our Cover." *Aldrichimica Acta* 18, 4 (1985),
p. 85, cover illus.

Bauch 1966
Bauch, K. *Rembrandt: Gemälde*. Berlin, 1966.

Beck 1973
Beck, H.-U. *Jan van Goyen, 1596–1656,* vol. 2: *Katalog der
Gemälde*. Amsterdam, 1973.

Beck 1991
Beck, H.-U. *Künstler um van Goyen: Maler und Zeichner*.
Doornspijk, 1991.

Bell 1899
Bell, M. *Rembrandt van Rijn and His Work*. London, 1899.

Benesch 1935–70
Benesch, O. *Rembrandt. Werk und Forschung*. Additions and
corrections by Eva Benesch. Lucerne, 1970.

Bernt 1970
Bernt, W. *The Netherlandish Painters of the Seventeenth
Century*. 3 vols. London, 1970.

Bialostocki 1984
Bialostocki, J. "A New Look at Rembrandt Iconography."
Artibus et Historiae 10 (1984), pp. 9–19.

Bialostocki and Wallicki 1957
Bialostocki, J. and M. Wallicki. *Europäische Malerei in
polnischen Sammlungen: 1300–1800.* Warsaw, 1957.

Bierman 1912
Bierman, G. "Die Gemäldesammlung des Baron Herzog
in Budapest." *Cicerone* 4 (1912), pp. 417–34.

Bode 1886
Bode, W. von. "Aus osterreichischen Galerien."
Repertorium für Kunstwissenschaft 9 (1886), pp. 309ff.

Bode 1890
Bode, W. von. Review of exhibition Berlin 1890. *Jahrbuch
der Königlich Preussischen Kunstsammlungen* 11 (1890),
pp. 199–241.

Bode and Hofstede de Groot 1897–1906
Bode, W. von. assisted by C. Hofstede de Groot.
The Complete Work of Rembrandt. 8 vols. Paris, 1897–1906.

Bol 1973
Bol, J. J. *Die holländische Marinemalerei des 17. Jahrhunderts*.
Braunschweig, 1973.

Bredius and Gerson 1969
Bredius, A. *Rembrandt*. 2nd ed., rev. H. Gerson. Oxford, 1969.

Brockwell 1920
Brockwell, M. *A Catalogue of Paintings in the Collection of
Mr. and Mrs. Charles P. Taft*. New York, 1920.

Broos 1994
Broos, B. *The Mauritshuis*. The Hague, 1994.

Brown 1907
Brown, G. Baldwin. *Rembrandt: A Study of His Life and
Work*. London and New York, 1907.

Bruyn 1987
Bruyn, J. "Towards a Scriptural Reading of Seventeenth-
Century Dutch Landscape Painting." In *Amsterdam,
1987–88*.

Buijsen 1998
Buijsen, E. *Haagse Schilders in de Gouden Eeuw. Het
Hoogsteder Lexikon van alle schilders werkzaam in Den Haag
1600–1700*. The Hague, 1998.

Burlington 1924 and 1925
Burlington Magazine. Illus. by Bachstitz Gallery, December
1924, p. iv and October 1925, p. vi.

Büttner and Unverfehrt 1993
Büttner, N. and G. Unverfehrt. *Jacob van Ruisdael in
Bentheim. Ein niederländischer Maler und die Burg Bentheim
im 17. Jahrhundert*. Bielefeld, 1993.

Cavalli-Björkman 1990
Cavalli-Björkman, G. *Illustrated Catalogue: European
Paintings*. Stockholm: Nationalmuseum, 1990.

Chiarini 1989
Chiarini, M. *I dipinti olandese del seicento e del settecento*.
Florence: Galerie e Musei Statali di Firenze, 1989.

Davies 1978
Davies, A. I. *Allart van Everdingen*. New York and London,
1978.

Davies 2001
Davies, A. I. *Allart van Everdingen 1621–1675: First Painter
of Scandinavian Landscape. Catalogue Raisonné of Paintings*.
Doornspijk, 2001.

Drost 1926
Drost, W. *Barockmalerei in den germanischen Ländern*.
Wildpark-Potsdam, 1926.

Dutuit 1884–85
Dutuit, E. *L'Oeuvre complet de Rembrandt*. Vol. 3 and supplement. *Tableaux et dessins de Rembrandt: Catalogue his-
torique et descriptif*. Paris, 1985.

Eisler 1918
Eisler, M. *Rembrandt als Landschafter*. Munich, 1918.

van Gelder 1948
van Gelder, J. G. "Rembrandt en het landschap."
In *Rembrandt*. Amsterdam, 1946, pp. 1–60.

Gerson 1936
Gerson, H. *Philips Koninck*. Berlin, 1936.

Gerson 1956
Gerson, H. "Rembrandt in Poland." *Burlington Magazine* 98
(1956), pp. 279–83.

Gerson 1968
Gerson, H. *Rembrandt Paintings*. London, 1968.

Giltaij 1992
Giltaij, J. "The problem of Isaack van Ruisdael (1599–1667)."
Burlington Magazine 134 (1992), pp. 180–82.

Haak 1969
Haak, B. *Rembrandt: His Life, His Work, His Time*. New York,
1969.

Hamann 1969
Hamann, R. *Rembrandt*. Rev. ed. Berlin, 1969.

Haverkorn van Rijsewijk 1901
Haverkorn van Rijsewijk, P. "Willem van de Velde de Oude."
Oud Holland 19 (1901), pp. 61–63.

Hoetink 1985
Hoetink, H. R. *The Royal Picture Gallery, Mauritshuis*.
New York and The Hague, 1985.

Hofstede de Groot 1907–27
Hofstede de Groot, C. *Beschreibendes und kritisches Verzeichnis der Werke der hervorragendsten holländischen Maler des XVII. Jahrhunderts.* 10 vols. Esslingen and Paris, 1907–27.

Hofstede de Groot 1908–27
Hofstede de Groot, C. *Catalogue Raisonné of the Work of the Most Eminent Dutch Painters Based on the Work of John Smith.* Trans. E. G. Houlle. 10 vols. London, 1908–27.

Hofstede de Groot 1909
Hofstede de Groot, C. "Nieuw-ontdeckte Rembrandts." *Onze Kunst* 8 (1909), pp. 10ff.

Hofstede de Groot 1912
Hofstede de Groot, C. "Nieuw-ontdeckte Rembrandts." *Onze Kunst* 22 (1912), pp. 137–88.

Hofstede de Groot and Valentiner 1913
Hofstede de Groot, C. and Valentiner, W. R. *Pictures in the Collection of P. A. B. Widener.* Privately printed, 1913.

Hollstein 1949
Hollstein, F. W. H. *The New Dutch and Flemish Etchings, Engravings and Woodcuts, c. 1450–1700.* Amsterdam, 1949.

Houbraken 1717–21
Houbraken, A. *De Groote Schouburgh der Nederlantsche Konstschilders en Schilderessen.* 3 vols. Amsterdam, 1717–21.

Huys Janssen 2001
Huys Janssen, P. Review of Davies 2001. *Burlington Magazine* 148 (November 2001), pp. 701–702.

Knuttel 1956
Knuttel, G. *Rembrandt: De Meester en zijn werk.* Amsterdam, 1956.

Larsen 1983
Larsen, E. *Rembrandt, peintre de paysages: Une vision nouvelle.* Louvain-la-neuve, 1983.

LaWall Lipshultz 1988
LaWall Lipshultz, S. *Selected Works: The Minneapolis Institute of Arts.* Minneapolis, 1988.

Le Bihan 1990
Le Bihan, O. *L'Or et L'Ombre: catalogue critique et raisonné des peintures du dix-sixième et du dix-septième siècle conservées au Musée des Beaux-Arts de Bordeaux.* Bordeaux: Musée des Beaux-Arts de Bordeaux, 1990.

MacLaren 1960
MacLaren, N. *National Gallery Catalogues: The Dutch School.* London: The National Gallery, 1960.

MacLaren 1991
MacLaren, N. *National Gallery Catalogues: The Dutch School, 1600–1900.* 2nd ed., rev. C. Brown. 2 vols. London: The National Gallery, 1991.

Martin 1935–36
Martin, W. *De Hollandsche Schilderkunst in de Zeventiende Eeuw.* 2 vols. Amsterdam, 1935–36.

Michel 1894
Michel, E. *Rembrandt: His Life, His Work, His Time.* Trans. Florence Simmonds. 2 vols. London, 1894.

Miedema 1980
Miedema, H. *De archiefbescheiden van de St Lukasgilde te Haarlem.* 2 vols. Alphen aan de Rijn (Canaletto), 1980.

Mireur 1911–12
Mireur, H. *Dictionnaire des ventes d'art faites en France et à l'étranger pendant les XVIIIme & XIXme siècles.* Paris, 1911–12.

Nannen 1985
Nannen, H. *Ludolf Backhuysen.* Emden, 1985.

Neumann 1922
Neumann, C. *Rembrandt.* Munich, 1922.

Preston 1937
Preston, L. R. *Sea and River Painters of the Netherlands in the Seventeenth Century.* London, 1937.

Preston 1974
Preston, L. R. *The Seventeenth Century Marine Painters of the Netherlands.* Leigh-on-Sea, 1974.

Raleigh 1956
Rembrandt and His Pupils. Cat. by W. R. Valentiner, Raleigh: North Carolina Museum of Art, 1956.

Raupp 1980
Raupp, H. J. "Zur Bedeutung von Thema und Symbol für die holländische Landschaftsmalerei des 17. Jahrhunderts." *Jahrbuch der Staatlichen Kunstsammlungen in Baden-Württemberg* 17 (1980), pp. 85–110.

van Regteren Altena 1967
Regteren Altena, I. Q. van. Review of Bauch 1966. *Oud Holland* 82 (1967), pp. 69–71.

Rembrandt Documents
Strauss, W. L. and M. van der Meulen, eds. *The Rembrandt Documents.* New York, 1979.

Rembrandt-Forschung 1957
"Die Rembrandt-Forschung im Lichte der Ausstellungen des Jahres 1956." *Kunstchronik* 10 (1957), pp. 117ff.

Rembrandt Research Project 1983–
Bruyn, J. et al. *A Corpus of Rembrandt Paintings.* The Hague, 1983–.

Robinson 1958–74
Robinson, M. S. *Van de Velde Drawings: A Catalogue of Drawings in the National Maritime Museum Made by the Elder and the Younger Willem van de Velde.* Cambridge, 1958–74.

Robinson 1990
Robinson, M. S. *The Paintings of Willem van de Velde.* London, 1990.

Rosenberg 1900
Rosenberg, A. *Adriaen und Isack van Ostade.* Bielefeld, 1900.

Rosenberg 1906
Rosenberg, A. *Rembrandt: Des Meisters Gemälde.* Stuttgart and Leipzig, 1906.

Rosenberg 1928
Rosenberg, J. *Jacob van Ruisdael.* Berlin, 1928.

Rosenberg 1948
Rosenberg, J. *Rembrandt: Life & Work.* Oxford, 1948.

Rosenberg, Slive, and Ter Kuile 1966
Rosenberg, J., S. Slive, and E. H. ter Kuile. *Dutch Art and Architecture, 1600 to 1800.* Pelican History of Art. Harmondsworth, 1966.

Rostworowski 1978
Rostworowski, M. *Rembrandta przpowiesc o milosiernym Samarytaninie* (Rembrandt's *Landscape with the Good Samaritan*). Cracow, 1978.

Roy 1972
Roy, R. "Studien zu Gerbrand van den Eeckhout." Ph.D. diss., Universität Wien, Vienna, 1972.

Saur 1999–
Saur Allgemeines Künstlerlexikon, Munich, 1999–.

Schatborn 2001
Schatborn, P. *Drawn to Warmth: 17th-century Dutch Artists in Italy.* Amsterdam and Zwolle, 2001.

Schmidt-Degener 1935
Schmidt-Degener, F. "Rembrandt's tegenstrijdigheden." In Amsterdam 1935.

Schmidt-Degener 1950
Schmidt-Degener, F. *Rembrandt.* Amsterdam, 1950.

Schnackenburg 1981
Schnackenburg, B. *Adriaen van Ostade, Isack van Ostade. Zeichnungen und Aquarelle. Gesamtdarstellung mit Werkkatalogen.* 2 vols. Hamburg, 1981.

Schneider 1985
Schneider, C. "A New Look at the *Landscape with an Obelisk.*" *Fenway Court,* June 1985.

Schneider 1990
Schneider, C. , *Rembrandt's Landscapes.* New Haven and London, 1990.

Schwartz 1985
Schwartz, G. *Rembrandt: His Life, His Paintings.* New York, 1985.

Slive 1953
Slive, S. *Rembrandt and His Critics, 1630–1730.* The Hague, 1953.

Slive 1995
Shop Talk: Studies in Honor of Seymour Slive: Presented on his Seventy-fifth Birthday. C. P. Schneider, W. W. Robinson and A. I. Davies, eds. Cambridge, 1995.

Slive 1998
Slive, S. "The Dutch Pelican I and II." *Simiolus* 26 (1998) pp. 179–86.

Slive 2001

Slive, S. *Jacob van Ruisdael: A Complete Catalogue of his Paintings, Drawings and Etchings.* New Haven, 2001.

Smith 1829–37

Smith, J. *A Catalogue Raisonné of the Works of the Most Eminent Dutch, Flemish, and French Painters.* 9 vols. London, 1829–37 (supplement 1842).

Stechow 1966

Stechow, W. *Dutch Landscape Painting of the 17th Century.* London, 1966.

Sullivan 1995

Sullivan, E. J., ed. *The Taft Museum: European and American Paintings.* Cincinnati,1995.

Sumowski 1979–92

Sumowski, W. *Drawings of the Rembrandt School.* 10 vols. New York, 1979–92.

Sumowski 1983–94

Sumowski, W. *Gemälde der Rembrandt-Schüler.* 6 vols. Landau, 1983–94.

Sutton 1986

Sutton, P. C. *A Guide to Dutch Art in America.* Washington, D.C., 1986.

Thieme-Becker 1907–50

Thieme, U. and F. Becker. *Allgemeines Lexikon der bildenden Künstler von der Antike bis zur Gegenwart.* 37 vols. Leipzig, 1907–50.

Tümpel 1986

Tümpel, C. *Rembrandt.* Belgium, 1986.

Valentiner 1908

Valentiner, W. R. *Rembrandt.* 3d ed. Stuttgart and Berlin, 1908.

Valentiner 1923

Valentiner, W. R. *Wiedergefundene Gemälde (1910–1920).* Klassiker der Kunst in Gesamtausgabe 27. 2nd rev. ed., Stuttgart and Berlin, 1923.

Veth 1941

Veth, J. *Rembrandts leven en kunst.* Amsterdam, 1941.

Vosmaer 1877

Vosmaer, C. *Rembrandt: Sa vie et ses oeuvres.* The Hague, 1877.

de Vries 1956

de Vries, A. B. *Rembrandt.* Baarn, 1956.

Walford 1991

Walford, J. *Jacob van Ruisdael and the Perception of Landscape.* New Haven, 1991.

Weisbach 1926

Weisbach, W. *Rembrandt.* Berlin and Leipzig, 1926.

Wheelock 1995

Wheelock, A. K. *Dutch Paintings of the Seventeenth Century.* Washington, D. C.: National Gallery of Art, 1995.

White 1984

White, C. *Rembrandt.* New York, 1984.

White and Boon 1969

White, C. and K. Boon. *Rembrandt Etchings. An Illustrated Critical Catalogue.* 2 vols. Amsterdam and New York, 1969.

Wijnmann 1932

Wijnmann, H. F. "Het leven der Ruysdaels." *Oud Holland* 49 (1932), pp. 49–60, 173–81, 258–75.

Willis 1911

Willis, F. C. *Die Niederländischen Marinemalerei.* Leipzig, 1911.

Zaluski 1956

Zaluski, A. "Le Paysage avec le Bon Samaritain de Rembrandt au Musée National de Cracovie et le problème de son expression." *Biuletyin historii szutki* 18 (1956), pp. 370–83.

Ziemba 1987

Ziemba, A. "Rembrandts Landschaft als Sinnbild: Versuch einer ikonologischen Deutung." *Artibus et Historiae* 15 (1987), pp. 109–34.

EXHIBITION CATALOGUES

Amsterdam 1983

Landscapes by Rembrandt and His Precursors. Cat. by Peter Schatborn. Amsterdam, Museum het Rembrandthuis, 1983.

Amsterdam 1985

Ludolf Backhuizen 1631–1708. Cat. by B. Broos, R. Vorstman, and W. L. Van de Wetering. Amsterdam: Rijksmuseum, 1985.

Amsterdam/Boston/Philadelphia 1987–88

Masters of 17th-Century Dutch Landscape Painting. Cat. by P. C. Sutton and P. J. J. van Thiel, with A. Blankert, J. Bruyn, C. J. de Bruyn Kops, A. Chong, J. Giltaij, S. Schama, and M. E. Wiesman. Amsterdam: Rijksmuseum; Boston: Museum of Fine Arts; and Philadelphia Museum of Art, 1987–88.

Berlin 1890

Katalog der Ausstellung von Werken der niederländischen Kunst des siebzehnten Jahrhunderts. Gemälde der holländischen und flämischen Schule, delfter Fayencen, Möbeln und Gegenständen der Kleinkunst im Berliner Privatbesitz. Berlin: Kunstgeschichtliche Gesellschaft in Berlin, 1890.

Berlin 1906

Ausstellung von Werken alter Kunst aus dem Privatbesitz der Mitglieder des Kaiser Friedrich-Museum-Vereins. Berlin (former Gräflich Redern'schen Palais), 1906.

Berlin/Amsterdam/London 1991–92

Rembrandt: Der Meister und seine Werkstatt/ De Meester en zijn Werkplaats/The Master and his Workshop. Vol. 1: *Gemälde/Schilderijen/Paintings.* Cat. by C.Brown, J. Kelch, V. Manuih, B. Schnackenburg, P. van Theil and others; vol. 2: *Zeichnungen und Radierungen/Tekeningen en Etsen/ Drawings and Etchings.* Cat. by H. Bevers, P. Schatborn, and B. Wetzel. Berlin: Gemäldegalerie and Kupferstichkabinett SMPK; Amsterdam: Rijksmuseum; and London: The National Gallery, 1991–92.

Boston/Chicago 2003–2004

Rembrandt's Journey: Prints, Drawings and Paintings. Cat. by C. S. Ackley, R. Baer, T. E. Rassieur, and W. W. Robinson. Boston: Museum of Fine Arts; and Chicago: The Art Institute of Chicago, 2003–2004.

Greenwich 1982

The Art of the Van de Veldes. Cat. by D. Cordingly. Greenwich, National Maritime Museum, 1982.

Kassel/Amsterdam 2001–2002

The Mystery of the Young Rembrandt. Cat. by E. van de Wetering, and B. Schnackenburg, eds. Kassel: Staatliche Museen Kassel, Gemäldegalerie Alte Meister, Schloss Wilhelmshöhe; and Amsterdam: Museum het Rembrandthuis, 2001–2002.

Kingston 2003

Gift of Genius: A Rembrandt for Kingston. Cat. by D. de Witt. Kingston: Agnes Etherington Art Centre, 2003.

London 1893

Spring Exhibition. London: Whitechapel (St. Jude's), 1893.

London 1953

Rembrandt and His Influence. London: Matthiesen Gallery, 1953.

London 2002

Inspired by Italy: Dutch Landscape Painting 1600–1700. Cat. by L. B. Harwood. London: Dulwich Picture Gallery, 2002.

Melbourne 1997

Rembrandt: A Genius and His Impact. Cat. by A. Blankert. Melbourne: National Gallery of Victoria, 1997.

Milwaukee 1976

The Bible Through Dutch Eyes: From Genesis Through the Apocrypha. Cat. by Alfred Bader. Milwaukee: Milwaukee Art Center, 1976.

Minneapolis/Toledo/Los Angeles 1990–91

Mirror of Empire: Dutch Marine Art of the Seventeenth Century. Cat. by G. S. Keyes, D. De Vries, J. A. Weln, and C. K. Wilson. Minneapolis: The Minneapolis Insitute of Arts; Toledo: The Toledo Museum of Art; and Los Angeles: Los Angeles County Museum of Art, 1990–91.

New York 1995

Old Master Paintings. New York: Otto Naumann Fine Arts, 1995.

Paris 1989

Eloge de la Navigation Hollandaise au XVIIe Siècle. Cat. by M. Berge-Gerbaud. Paris: Institut Néerlandais, Fondation Custodia, 1989.

Raleigh 1956

Rembrandt and His Pupils. Cat. by W. R. Valentiner. Raleigh: North Carolina Museum of Art, 1956.

Washington/Los Angeles 2005

Rembrandt's Late Religious Portraits. Cat. by A. K. Wheelock. Washington, D. C.: National Gallery of Art; and Los Angeles: The J. Paul Getty Museum, 2005.